Nutritional Guidelines Used for the Take Care of Yourself Menu Program

The American Heart Association recommends that adults limit their total fat intake to approximately 25-30% of calories consumed and limit cholesterol to less than 300 mg daily.

The guidelines for this program assume that an adult eats approximately 2000 calories per day with 400 calories being consumed at breakfast, 800 calories consumed at lunch and 800 calories consumed at supper. Since low-fat side dishes will be served along with the chosen entree, the fat content of the entree may exceed 30%. Each entree does not exceed:

350 Calories
16 Grams of Fat
1000 mg Sodium
90 mg Cholesterol

Side dishes served will include:

Tossed Salad (dressing?)
1/2 cup Vegetable (without margarine/oil)
Dinner Roll with 1 Tbsp. margarine
LowFat Dessert

If desired, 1 cup of pasta may be used and the dinner roll is omitted.

If you listen closely turning these pages, you can almost hear Chef Andrea and the rest of Italy enjoying the last laugh. Imagine the sheer joy of watching the world discover (or rediscover) that its favorite cuisine is also one of its very healthiest. With this collection of useful tips and dazzlingly direct recipes, Chef Andrea opens the door even wider to those who seek Italian warmth, pleasure and sheer sunshine within the context of a lifestyle both moderate and modern.

John DeMers
Food and Wine Editor
New Orleans Magazine

DEDICATION. . .

To my dear wife Cathie who has been the love of my life and has inspired me and helped me in becoming successful, I lovingly dedicate this book.

I would also like to dedicate this book to my dear brother Lauro Apuzzo who was like a father to me. He always stood by me and helped me throughout my career.

Dear Chef Andrea,

Please accept my most sincere expressions of commendation and gratitude to you for producing this most impressive cook book dedicated not only to delicious dishes but also to good dietary practices.

You have achieved a triumph in the culinary world of providing accomplished chefs and cooking neophytes alike with an easy to follow encyclopedic offering of basic classical recipes composed of healthful ingredients and of your own famous Andrea dishes.

Perhaps the most important contribution is your detailed account of the step by step procedures in the making of basic stocks and sauces that are essential to culinary success.

Thank you for sharing your knowledge, your love and your skill in creating these magnificent recipes.

Sincerely,
Lindy Boggs

Foreword

*O*ver the past five years, I have had the pleasure of being a "regular" at Andrea Apuzzo's fabulous northern Italian restaurant in the New Orleans suburb of Metairie, Louisiana. During that time, I have had the opportunity to bring friends, family and professional associates to share this talented chef's cuisine. On all occasions, there has never been a moment when the quality of his wide variety of dishes has been anything less than outstanding. The secret to Andrea's success, as I am sure all who know his restaurant will agree, is his intense personal involvement in both his kitchen and his customers. The service provided by his capable staff reflect the role model set by Andrea himself.

As one who is very appreciative of his Italian-American heritage, and also fortunate to have traveled through most of Italy over the past two decades, I learned early in my life the delights of Italian cuisine. I also recognized that many Americans have a very narrow view of "Italian Food", and often feel that it is "fattening". Indeed, it is surprising to many that the incidence of diseases of heart and circulation in Italy is much less than in the more northern, dairy producing countries of Europe. In fact, epidemiologists and medical experts in nutrition and fat metabolism now recognize and understand the tremendous benefits and advantages to the use of monounsaturated fats, such as olive oil, in preference to butter. Even garlic has achieved scientific recognition for its anti-thrombotic (blood clot prevention) qualities.

For those who have come to know northern Italian cuisine in particular, the vast spectrum of seafood, poultry, game, veal, beef and other dishes, as well as the manner in which Italians treat fruits and vegetables, truly opens up a world of culinary delights. Yet, pervading all Italian cuisine is an underlying principle of simplicity and beauty. To experience these qualities, one only has to come to Andrea's!

In his first cookbook published in 1989, Andrea made a gift to all of his fans by providing those of us who love to cook with the opportunity to share in his tremendous experience. While I believe that most all Italian dishes are intrinsically "healthy", Andrea has chosen to produce another treasure that focuses on "extra light" Italian recipes and he has honored me, as a cardiologist, by asking me to review his new cookbook.

I have studied each and every menu in detail and tried several in my own kitchen. In short, Andrea has put together a collection of marvelous recipes with particular attention to fat and overall caloric content. These dishes follow the principles of the American Heart Association to lower cholesterol context and overall fat consumption in this country but, at the same time, preserve the pleasure of true Italian cuisine.

By reading nutrition information labels on food products and by cooking from recipes which provide nutrition information, like the ones in this book, it will be easier to keep track of the number of grams of fat you are eating on a daily basis. Also, here are a few simple ways to help you cut back on fat in your own recipes at home:

1. Choose lean meat, fish and poultry.
2. Trim all excess fat from meat and skin your poultry.
3. Drain fat after cooking meats.
4. Choose low-fat or fat-free dairy products.
5. Bake, boil, or broil, instead of frying.
6. Moderate your use of animal source food products.
7. Read nutrition information labels.

I hope you enjoy these recipes as much as I have. Bueno Appetito!

Sharon Haggerty Taylor
Registered Dietitian

Introduction

My initial introduction to Chef Andrea occurred when I was the Director of the Ochsner Diabetes Institute at the Ochsner Clinic in New Orleans, Louisiana. Chef Andrea was my first guest chef in a series of heart healthy cooking classes, New Orleans style! It was after that first class that Chef Andrea approached me about co-authoring a low-fat Northern Italian cookbook to compliment his already famous cookbook, "La Cucina di Andrea's". Andrea's huge success can be attributed to his number one goal: to please the guest. That is the reason he created this book. At Andrea's Restaurant, he offers one of the largest menus in town, several deliciously fresh daily specials, and is always happy to prepare something special - like grilled fish with no butter, or sauce on the side – at the customer's request.

Now Andrea's Restaurant proudly offers a low-fat menu for lunch and dinner for those guests that prefer their meal "on the lighter side". The low-fat menu, as well as every recipe in this book provides you with nutrition information including the number of calories, grams of fat, and milligrams of sodium per serving.

These days most of us know we should cut down on the amount of fat we eat. But most people are confused about how much fat should be in their daily diet. No diet should be without fat, as fat is a very important nutrient. Fat provides our bodies with a concentrated source of energy. In addition, fat carries important vitamins and helps to make our food taste good. The American Heart Association and the American Dietetic Association both agree that no more than 30% of your daily caloric intake should come from fat and that less than 10% of saturated fats should make up your total fat. Here's a chart to help you determine how many grams of fat equal 30% of your total daily calorie intake.

Daily calorie intake	Grams of total fat consumed daily	Grams of saturated fat consumed daily
1200	40	13
1400	47	16
1600	53	18
2000	67	22
2200	73	24
2400	80	27
2600	87	29
2800	93	31
3000	100	33

Table of Contents

Appetizers

Carpaccio Of Tuna Or Salmon

Some might object to the fact that the fish is uncooked for this cold appetizer. In reality, the cooking is done not by heat but by the acidity of the marinade, which changes the texture of the fish completely.

3 oz. fresh yellowfin tuna or salmon, thinly sliced
1/2 celery stalk with leaves, chopped
1/8 onion, chopped
1/4 carrot, chopped
1/8 cup lemon juice
1/8 cup white wine
1 cup white vinegar
1/8 cup dry vermouth
1/4 tsp. salt
Pinch crushed red pepper

Sauce:
2 sprigs mint
4 stems dill
1/2 Tbs. extra virgin olive oil
1 Tbs. lemon juice
2 Tbs. white wine
1 Tbs. dry vermouth

1   Fan out thin slices of fish in a non-metallic dish. Combine the remaining ingredients and pour that liquid over the fish.

2   Marinate in refrigerator at least eight hours.

3   Place mint, dill, olive oil, wine, lemon juice and vermouth in a blender and puree the mixture until smooth.

4   Remove the fish from the marinade and serve with the lemon wine sauce.

Serves two.

NUTRITION INFORMATION PER SERVING
Tuna:
84 calories
3 gm. fat
Less than 1 gm. saturated fat
278 mg. sodium

Salmon:
112 calories
5 gm. fat
1 gm. saturated fat
184 mg. sodium

Carpaccio Of Beef

4 slices of filet mignon, about 1/8 inch thick (3 oz.)
1 Tbs. low-fat mayonnaise
1 1/2 Tbs. Dijon mustard
1/4 tsp. Tabasco
1/4 tsp. Worcestershire
1 Tbs. brandy
1/4 tsp. lemon juice

1 Place the filets, one at a time, between two large sheets of plastic. With the smooth side of a large meat mallet or the side of a heavy cleaver, pound the filets until they are about eight inches across and very thin. Carefully peel the meat away from the plastic, and arrange on a large serving plate.

2 Make the sauce by whisking together all the sauce ingredients. Squeeze one lemon wedge over the beef and top with the sauce. Garnish as desired.

Serves two.

NUTRITION INFORMATION PER SERVING
146 calories
5 gm. fat
Less than 1 gm. saturated fat
184 mg. sodium

Sauteed Mushrooms

1 tsp. margarine
1 Tbs. chopped onion
1/2 tsp. chopped garlic
10 large mushrooms, cut in quarters
1/3 cup white wine
Juice of one lemon
1/8 tsp. dried oregano

1 Heat the margarine in a skillet until it bubbles. Add the onion, garlic, and mushrooms, and cook until the onions turn soft.

2 Add the white wine, lemon juice and oregano. Simmer over medium heat until mushrooms have softened and most of the liquid is absorbed.
Serves four.

NUTRITIONAL INFORMATION PER SERVING
30 Calories
Less than 1 gm. fat
0 gm. of saturated fat
24 mg. sodium

Mozzarella Di Bufala Capricciosa

Buffalo-Milk Mozzarella Antipasto

8 oz. Buffalo-milk mozzarella
1 leaf chopped fresh basil
1 tsp. extra virgin olive oil
1/8 tsp. salt
pinch white pepper
1/2 tsp. balsamic vinegar
1 head Boston bibb lettuce

1 Slice the mozzarella into approximately 1/4 inch thick pieces.
2 Fan the slices out on a serving plate.
3 Combine all remaining ingredients and pour over the cheese.
    Serves two.

NUTRITIONAL INFORMATION PER SERVING
80 Calories
5 gm. fat
161 mg. sodium

Melanzane A Fungitelli

Eggplant Caponata Andrea

1/2 cup vegetable oil
3 medium eggplants, well washed
1/4 cup salt
1 lb. fresh plum tomatoes
1/4 cup extra virgin olive oil
3 cloves garlic, lightly crushed
1/4 tsp. crushed red pepper
1/2 tsp. chopped garlic
8 leaves fresh basil, chopped
Pinches of salt and pepper
1 sprig Italian parsley, chopped

1   Cut eggplants into one-inch dice. Sprinkle the eggplant with salt. Put the eggplant dice into a colander, arranging them in a relatively uniform layer up the sides. Put a bowl the same size of the colander inside the colander, and weigh it down with 3-4 pounds of weight. Put the entire apparatus into the sink for 45 minutes. This will remove the bitterness from the eggplant.

2   Rinse the salt off the eggplant with cold water. Drain it well, then rinse again. Shake excess water off, then place eggplant onto a very large, dry towel. It is very important that you get the eggplant as dry as possible, to avoid spattering when you saute.

3   In a large, deep skillet heat vegetable oil until hot. Brown garlic lightly, and then about half of the eggplant. Saute until golden brown—about two minutes. With a skimmer, remove first batch of eggplant and drain on paper towels. Keep the garlic in the pan and saute the remainder of the eggplant.

4   Cut the stem ends off of the tomatoes and cut the tomatoes in half. Squeeze the seeds out. Cut tomatoes coarsely.

5   Pour off any remaining oil and the crushed garlic cloves from the skillet. Add the extra virgin olive oil and heat until it ripples. Saute chopped garlic until light brown. Add crushed red pepper and tomatoes and saute over medium high heat for about a minute. Add 1/2 cup water and lower flame to medium heat. Reduce contents in skillet by half.

6   Add basil, a pinch of salt and pepper, and parsley to pan and stir. Add eggplant and heat through. Remove from heat and allow to cool. Serve at room temperature.

Serves 12 to 16 appetizers.

NUTRITIONAL INFORMATION PER SERVING
101 Calories
10 gm. fat
1 gm. of saturated fat
336 mg. sodium

Scarole Alla Scapece

Escarole With Raisins And Olives

3 heads escarole
1 Tbs. extra virgin olive oil
1/2 tsp. crushed red pepper
4 cloves garlic, crushed
2 Tbs. raisins
2 Tbs. black olives, pitted and crushed
1/2 tsp. salt
Pinch white pepper
4 anchovies, chopped
1 Tbs. pine nuts

1   Cut the heads of escarole into eight pieces top to bottom and pull apart. Put the leaves into a large bowl and wash three times with cold water. Escarole often has lot of dirt in it. Drain well and spin or towel dry.

2   Heat the olive oil until very hot in a large skillet. Saute the garlic with the crushed red pepper until garlic is lightly browned. Add the escarole and saute over low heat until leaves are limp but stems are still crisp. Add all other ingredients and cook until warmed through.

Serves 10-12 appetizers.

NUTRITION INFORMATION PER SERVING
40 calories
3 gm. fat
1 gm. saturated fat
100 mg. sodium

Peperonata Marinata

Marinated Bell Peppers

3 medium-large red bell peppers
3 medium-large green bell peppers
1 medium-large yellow or orange bell peppers
2 Tbs. extra virgin olive oil
3 cloves garlic, sliced (not chopped)
1/4 tsp. crushed red pepper
4 sprigs Italian parsley
1/4 tsp. salt
Pinch white pepper

1 Roast peppers under a hot broiler, turning to blacken about 75 percent of the outer surface of the peppers. (This also can be done by holding the peppers above the open flame on your stove with a fork.) Don't be shy about this; it will look like you're burning and ruining them, but you're bringing out the flavors of the peppers. After they are charred, let them cool.

2 Peel off the outer skin—both the charred parts and those that aren't. Pull off the stem end, which will have a lot of seeds attached; try to get most of them out. Split the pepper open and remove as many seeds as possible. Slice the peppers into strips about a half-inch wide.

3 Heat the olive oil in a saute pan till hot. Cook the garlic until browned around the edges. Lower the heat and add the crushed red pepper, parsley, salt, white pepper, and the bell peppers. Cook for about 15 seconds, combining the ingredients thoroughly and making sure the peppers are well-coated with the oil.

4 Remove the contents of the pan to a bowl and allow to cool. Serve at room temperature as an antipasto.

Serves 10 to 12 appetizers.

NUTRITION INFORMATION PER SERVING
35 calories
3 gm. fat
0 gm. saturated fat
83 mg. sodium

Carote Alla Mente

Carrots With Mint

3 large carrots
1 tsp. salt
4 sprigs fresh mint leaves, chopped
3 leaves fresh basil, chopped
1 Tbs. chopped onion
1/2 tsp. chopped garlic
2 Tbs. extra virgin olive oil
1/4 tsp. Tabasco
1/2 tsp. Worcestershire
1 sprig oregano leaves, chopped
1 Tbs. balsamic vinegar
1 tsp. white vinegar
Pinch salt
Pinch white pepper

1 Peel carrots and cut off tops. Slice carrots on a slight diagonal into coins about 1/8th inch thick.
2 Bring a gallon of water with one tsp. salt to a boil. Put the carrots in and cook for 7-10 minutes or until they are somewhat tender but still have a raw carrot taste. As soon as you remove the carrots from the boiling water, plunge them into ice water.
3 Combine all other ingredients into a bowl. Add the carrots and toss well with the sauce. Let the carrots marinate over night and serve with a garnish of lettuce or fresh herbs.
   Serves 8-10 appetizers.

NUTRITION INFORMATION PER SERVING
40 calories
3 gm. fat
0 gm. saturated fat
106 mg. sodium

Ostriche Alla Fiorentina

Oysters Florentine

2 lbs. fresh spinach, well washed and picked of large stems
10-12 sprigs Italian parsley leaves

White sauce:
1 Tbs. margarine
1/3 cup all-purpose flour
1 1/3 cups skimmed evaporated milk

1 Tbs. olive oil
1/2 green bell pepper, chopped
1 rib celery, chopped
5 cloves garlic, lightly crushed
1 large onion, chopped
1 cup fish stock
1/4 tsp. cayenne
1/4 tsp. nutmeg
1/2 tsp. salt
1/4 tsp. white pepper
2 Tbs. oyster water
1 Tbs. Sambuca liqueur
36 oysters, drained, water reserved

1   Preheat oven to 450 degrees.

2   Boil two quarts of water in a large saucepan. In it, poach the spinach for 2 minutes. Drain the spinach and wash with cold water. With your hands, squeeze the excess water out.

3   In a food processor, chop the spinach and the parsley together until fine but not pureed.

4   Melt the margarine in a medium skillet and when bubbling, sprinkle in the flour while whisking constantly. Whisk milk in with butter and flour and bring to a boil. Lower to a simmer for five minutes, whisking frequently, to make a thick, smooth white sauce.

5   Heat the olive oil in a large skillet over medium-high heat. Add bell pepper, celery, garlic, and onion. Cook until edges of onions begin to brown, stirring frequently.

6   Add fish stock. Bring to a boil and reduce by about a third. Stir in spinach-parsley mixture from food processor. Add cayenne and nutmeg.

7   Cook for three or four minutes over medium heat, stirring frequently, until excess liquid has been absorbed.

8   Stir in white sauce, salt, and white pepper. Cook until mixture begins to boil again, then remove to the food processor container. Add oyster water, and process into a course puree.

9   Return sauce to skillet. Pour Sambuca over the top and carefully flame it. Heat sauce until bubbles well up, then remove from heat. Allow to cool to lukewarm.

10   Place oysters on shells, in ramekins, or in small au gratin dishes. Top each oyster with a tablespoon of the sauce. If using shells, place them on a pie plate half-filled with rock salt.

11   Bake oysters in a preheated 450 degrees oven for 10 minutes or until tops are lightly browned.
12   Serve with a warning to your guests about how hot they are.
Serves six.

NUTRITION INFORMATION PER SERVING
148 calories
4 gm. fat
1 gm. saturated fat
383 mg. sodium

Mozzarella Capricciosa
Mozzarella Antipasto

8 oz. fresh skim-milk mozzarella
1 leaf chopped fresh basil
1 tsp. extra virgin olive oil
1/8 tsp. salt
Pinch white pepper
1/2 tsp. balsamic vinegar
1 head Boston or Bibb lettuce

1   Slice the mozzarella into approximately 1/4 inch thick pieces.
2   Fan the slices out on a serving plate.
3   Combine all remaining ingredients except lettuce and pour over the cheese.
Serves two.

NUTRITION INFORMATION PER SERVING
80 calories
5 gm. fat
2 gm. saturated fat
161 mg. sodium

Vitello Tonnato
Cold Roast Veal with Tuna Mayonnaise

1 1/4 lbs. white veal round
1 tsp. salt
1/8 tsp. white pepper
1 Tbs. vegetable oil
2 garlic cloves, lightly crushed
1/4 carrot, cut into coins
1/4 onion sliced
1 rib celery, chopped
1 cup dry white wine
1 bay leaf
1/2 tsp. dry rosemary

Sauce:
1 cup canned tuna, packed in water, well drained
   or 4 oz. fresh tuna, poached
4 anchovies
2 Tbs. small capers
1 1/2 tsp. minced garlic
1 Tbs. onions
1 cup low-fat mayonnaise
1 1/2 tsp. lemon juice
5 drops Tabasco
1/4 tsp. Worcestershire sauce

1   Preheat oven to 450 degrees.
2   Make sure that the veal round is trimmed of excess fat and peeled of its "silk."
3   Sprinkle the salt and pepper on the outside of the veal.
4   Heat the oil in a skillet and saute the garlic until browned around the edges.
5   Place the veal round in the skillet. Brown lightly on all sides. Put the entire skillet into a preheated 450 degrees oven and roast, basting and turning the veal about every five minutes.
6   After about 10 minutes in the oven, add the carrot, onion, and celery, and continue to cook, baste and turn for another 10 minutes.
7   Add white wine, bay leaf, and a cup of water. Cover skillet with aluminum foil and braise for five minutes, or until interior temperature is 140 degrees.
8   Remove veal from oven and discard other skillet contents. Cool veal to room temperature.
9   Meanwhile, make sauce by blending all sauce ingredients in a food processor until anchovies and capers have been beaten into small bits. Do not puree.
10   When veal is cool, slice thinly at a 45-degree angle. Arrange five slices on a plate, and put two tablespoons of the sauce in the center of the

plate. Garnish with strips of anchovy, individual capers, a sprig of rosemary, a wedge of lemon, and a slice of tomato. Serve cold.
Makes eight appetizers.

NUTRITION INFORMATION PER SERVING
218 calories
7 gm. fat
1 gm. saturated fat
269 mg. sodium

Salmone Affumicato
Smoked Salmon Dannon

1/2 tsp. fresh dill, chopped
1 tsp. Dijon mustard
1 cup low-fat yogurt
1/2 tsp. honey
1 1/2 oz. smoked salmon, sliced thin

1 In a saucepan, heat the yogurt under low heat to a smooth consistency. Remove from the heat and let cool.
2 Add mustard, dill, and honey.
3 Place salmon slices on a plate with the sauce on the side for dipping.
Serves one.

NUTRITION INFORMATION PER SERVING
210 calories
5 gm. fat
2 gm. saturated fat
560 mg. sodium

Yogurt Sauce

1 cup plain low-fat yogurt
2 Tbs. minced fresh mint
2 Tbs. lemon juice
1 tsp. minced garlic

Combine all ingredients in a bowl. Serve with seafood, vegetables or fresh fruit. It can be refrigerated for use with salads and cold appetizers.

NUTRITION INFORMATION PER SERVING
(Two-ounce serving)
19 calories
0 gm. fat
0 gm. saturated fat
20 mg. sodium

Vegetable Dip

1 cup low-fat yogurt
1/2 cup tomatoes, peeled, seeded, and chopped
2 Tbs. chopped scallions
2 Tbs. chopped parsley
2 Tbs. chopped celery
1 Tbs. chopped green pepper
Salt and pepper to taste
Tabasco to taste

Combine all the ingredients in a bowl. Serve with tortilla chips, sesame crackers, or vegetables.

NUTRITION INFORMATION PER SERVING
(Two-ounce serving)
21 calories
0 gm. fat
0 gm. saturated fat
70 mg. sodium

Basics

Fondo Bianco Di Vitello

Veal Stock For White Sauces

4 lbs. veal bones
2 ribs celery
1/2 large onion
8 cloves
1/2 leek, pulled apart and washed well
3 gallons water

Put these dry seasonings into a small cheesecloth bag ("sacchetto"):
1 tsp. black peppercorns
1 tsp. thyme
1 tsp. marjoram
1 tsp. rosemary
1/4 cup fresh parsley with stems, chopped
4 bay leaves

1 Remove the leaves from the celery (reserve for some other use) and cut ribs into one-inch pieces. Stud the onion half with the cloves. Clean the leek very well and chop off the roots.

2 Put all the ingredients into a large stockpot with three gallons of water and bring to a boil. Lower to a simmer and allow to simmer for three to four hours, until you have about half the original amount of water. (The longer you simmer, the stronger the stock will get, but reducing it by half gives the strength of stock we will be using in all the other recipes in this book). Skim the scum off the top of the pot as it simmers (this is mostly fat).

3 When the stock has reached the right concentration, strain it through a large sieve. Refrigerate the stock in a large open container.

4 Any fat that remains will float to the top and congeal, so you can remove it easily. Store the stock in closed containers.
Makes a gallon and a half of stock.

NUTRITION INFORMATION PER QUART
36 calories
Less than 1 gm. fat
0 gm. saturated fat
74 mg. sodium

Fondo Bruno Di Carne

Beef Stock

6 lbs. beef bones, not cut or broken
1 medium onion
6 cloves
6 ribs celery
1 large carrot
Stems only from one bunch parsley
8-10 bay leaves
1 tsp. dried thyme
1/2 cup tomato, chopped
4 gallons water

Put these dry seasonings into a small cheesecloth bag ("sacchetto"):
1 tsp. black peppercorns
1 tsp. thyme
1 tsp. marjoram
1 tsp. rosemary
1/4 cup fresh parsley with stems, chopped
4 bay leaves

1   Boil four gallons of water in a large stockpot. Meanwhile, slice the onion (don't peel it) in half, and place the halves cut side down in a hot black iron skillet or on a griddle. Leave them there until the downside of the onion gets black. This will caramelize the sugars in the onion and also lend a little color. Stud the onion with the cloves.

2   Put all the ingredients into the stockpot and proceed as instructed for the veal stock. You will note that this stock will take on a light brown color as it simmers in contrast to the very pale color of the other two stocks.

Makes one and a half gallons of stock.

NUTRITION INFORMATION PER QUART
36 calories
Less than 1 gm. fat
0 gm. saturated fat
74 mg. sodium

Salsa Di Base Bruna
Demi-Glace

6 lbs. veal bones
1 large carrot, coarsely chopped
1 medium onion, coarsely chopped
4 ribs celery, leaves removed, coarsely chopped
6 cloves garlic, coarsely chopped
1/4 cup tomato paste
1 quart dry red wine
1 cup all-purpose flour
6 gallons water, total
6 cherry tomatoes, cut in half (or one regular tomato, cut up)
10-12 parsley stems

Put these dry seasonings into a small cheesecloth bag ("sacchetto"):
1 1/2 Tbs. black peppercorns
1 1/2 Tbs. dry rosemary leaves
1 tsp. dry sage
1 Tbs. thyme leaves
1 Tbs. marjoram

1 With a heavy cleaver, split bones into two inch pieces (you can ask your butcher to do this for you). Load bones into a baking pan. Put the pan on top of the stove over high heat first to heat the bones up quickly. Then, put the pan of bones into a 500 degrees oven. Every 10 minutes shuffle bones around in pan.

2 Meanwhile, make a mirepoix by chopping the carrot, celery, onion, and garlic coarsely and mixing together.

3 When the edges of the meat start to turn black (about 25-30 minutes), lower oven to 450 degrees and scatter the mirepoix around in the pan. Mix the bones and the mirepoix well, and return to the oven.

4 After about five minutes mix tomato paste into pan. Return to oven another five minutes then add red wine. When wine has reduced to about half the original quantity, add one quart of water and stir pan well.

5 After the bones have been in the oven for about an hour total, sprinkle flour over pan contents and stir well. Immediately load contents of pan into a large stockpot. Pour half a gallon of water into the pan, scraping the bottom and sides. Pour this water from the pan, along with another three gallons of water, into the stockpot.

6 Add the sacchetto. Put the stockpot over a hot fire and bring to a boil. Skim top of pot occasionally to remove scum and fat.

7 After about three hours add tomatoes and parsley stems to pot. After stock is reduced by half, add two more gallons of cold water. Continue to simmer and skim.

8 Reduce to half or even more, depending on the intensity of the demi-

Pork Sauce

1/8 cup vegetable oil
2 lbs. pork bones
1 medium carrot, cut up
1 medium onion, cut up
1 rib celery, cut up
2 cloves garlic, lightly crushed
1/4 cup tomato paste (no added salt)
1 cup dry white wine
1/2 cup flour
3 bay leaves
8-10 parsley stems
1 Tbsp. salt
pinch white pepper

1   Heat the vegetable oil in a large saucepan or dutch oven till very hot. Put in the pork bones, carrots, onions, celery and garlic. Brown everything for about five minutes.

2   Raise the heat to high and stir the tomato paste and one cup of wine into the pan. Sprinkle the flour around the pan and stir well. When browned, add a gallon of cold water and stir well. Scrape up all the burned parts that have stuck to the pan. Add bay leaves, parsley stems, salt and pepper. Bring the sauce to a boil, then reduce heat to a simmer.

3   The sauce is done after cooking for an hour, and reduced by one-half. Strain the sauce through a sieve.

Makes 3-4 cups depending on how far the volume is reduced upon cooking.

NUTRITIONAL INFORMATION PER SERVING
168 Calories
7 gm. fat
0 mg. cholesterol
605 mg. sodium

glace you want. Strain the demi-glace through fine cheesecloth. Skim off any remaining fat. Reserve demi-glace in refrigerator until ready to use. It will keep from a week to two weeks. It can also be frozen.

Makes two quarts.

NUTRITION INFORMATION PER QUART
668 calories
3 gm. fat
2 gm. saturated fat
375 mg. sodium

Fondo Bruno Di Pollame

Chicken Stock

4 lbs. chicken (either whole chickens or leftover pieces like backbones, etc.)
2 ribs celery
1/2 onion
4 cloves
4-5 leeks (green tops only)
1 tsp. salt
3 gallons water

Put these dry seasonings into a small cheesecloth bag (''sacchetto''):
1 tsp. black peppercorns
1 tsp. thyme
1 tsp. marjoram
1 tsp. rosemary
1/4 cup fresh parsley with stems, chopped
4 bay leaves

This procedure is exactly the same as for the veal stock, except use only two gallons of water. You will note that the chicken stock will throw off a lot less scum but a lot more fat. This should be thoroughly removed.

Makes one and a half gallons of stock.

NUTRITION INFORMATION PER QUART
35 calories
Less than 1 gm. fat
0 gm. saturated fat
74 mg. sodium

Fondo Bianco Di Gamberi

Shrimp Stock

1 lb. shrimp shells and heads
1 medium carrot, peeled and cut into chunks
2 sticks celery, cut up
1 tsp. salt
2 gallons water

Put these dry seasonings into a small cheesecloth bag ("sacchetto"):
1 Tbs. black peppercorns
1 Tbs. dried thyme
1 Tbs. oregano
1 Tbs. dried basil
5 stems of fresh dill or (one tsp. dried dill)
1/2 tsp. dried sage
4 bay leaves
1 tsp. marjoram
2 sprigs parsley

1   Put the shrimp shells and heads, onion, carrot, and celery into a soup pot with two gallons of cold water. Over medium high heat, bring to a boil. Add the sacchetto.

2   Boil the stock gently for one hour, then add the salt and remove from the heat.

Makes one and a half gallons of stock.

NUTRITION INFORMATION PER QUART
15 calories
0 gm. fat
0 gm. saturated fat
402 mg. sodium

Fondo Bianco Di Pesce

Fish Stock

5 lbs. fish heads, skins, bones, etc. (omit livers and gills)
2 ribs celery, coarsely chopped
1 whole medium onion, cut into chunks
2 bay leaves
1 whole leek, cut up
1 tsp. salt
2 gallons water

Put these dry seasonings into a small cheesecloth bag ("sacchetto"):
1 tsp. black peppercorns
1/2 Tbs. dried thyme
1/2 Tbs. dried oregano
1/2 Tbs. dried marjoram

1   The fish bones throw off a lot of scum, so I always pre-boil them before starting the stock. Put the fish bones in a stock pot and cover them with water. Bring the pot to a boil for five minutes. Then drain off all the water and rinse the fish bones with cold water. Drain that water off, too.

2   Now add two gallons of water to begin really making the stock. Put in all the vegetables and seasonings and bring to a boil. Let the pot boil briskly for five minutes then lower the fire to medium heat. Simmer for 90 minutes or until you have a little more than half the volume you started with. Skim the foam now and then during the cooking.

3   When the reduction is complete, strain the stock through a large sieve or china cap. This stock has the flavor strength I find most useful in my kitchen. Of course, you can continue to reduce it to make it stronger. It will keep in the refrigerator for about a week. You can also freeze it for use as needed.

Makes one and a half gallons of stock.

NUTRITION INFORMATION PER QUART
15 calories
0 gm. fat
0 gm. saturated fat
402 mg. sodium

Soup

Crema Di Carciofi
Artichoke Soup

8 medium artichokes
1/2 cup lemon juice
1 Tbs. margarine
2 ribs celery, cut up
1 medium onion, cut up
1 potato, peeled and sliced
1/2 cup dry white wine
3 quarts chicken stock
2 bay leaves
1/2 cup skimmed evaporated milk
1/2 tsp. salt
Pinch white pepper

1   Soak the artichokes overnight in a gallon of water with the lemon juice. From each artichoke, trim off and reserve a half-inch or a little more off the top, a half-inch off the bottom (including the stem), and the outer two layers of leaves. The trimmings are what you use to make the soup. (Save the tender, trimmed artichokes for steaming, stuffing, or antipasto. To keep them fresh, store them covered with water with some lemon juice).

2   In a large saucepan, heat the margarine to bubbling and in it saute the celery and onions until the onions turn translucent.

3   Add the potatoes and artichoke trimmings. Cook over medium fire for about five minutes until the artichoke leaves become tender. Add the wine and bring to a boil. Then add the stock, three quarts of water, and the bay leaves. Boil, then lower heat and simmer for two hours or until everything is very tender.

4   Strain soup through a sieve. Remove the bay leaves. Put the rest of the soup solids into a food processor and make a course puree. Add this back into the strained soup. Strain the soup again through a course sieve to remove the stringy parts of the artichokes.

5   Return the soup to a simmer. Stir in skimmed evaporated milk and add salt and pepper to taste. I prefer to keep my soups light in texture. However, you can thicken this soup by simmering it longer.

Serves eight.

NUTRITION INFORMATION PER SERVING
77 calories
Less than 1 gm. fat
0 gm. saturated fat
125 mg. sodium

Zuppa D'Aglio

Garlic Soup

3 heads fresh garlic
1 Tbs. olive oil
1 medium-large onion, cut up
2 ribs celery, cut up
1 cup dry white wine
1/4 cup all-purpose flour
1 gallon chicken stock
1 medium potato, peeled and cut-up
1 cup skim evaporated milk
10 chopped fresh basil leaves
1 sprig fresh thyme leaves, chopped
1/4 tsp. salt
1/4 tsp. white pepper
1/2 tsp. Tabasco

1 Cut two of the garlic heads in half across and remove the papery outer skin. Put these cut side down on a very hot skillet or griddle until they're black. Peel all the garlic completely, and crush the unblackened cloves.

2 Heat the olive oil in a large saucepan and saute the onions, celery, and the crushed garlic until lightly browned at the edges. Add the wine and bring to a boil.

3 Sprinkle in the flour and stir the pot thoroughly, but don't let it brown. Add the chicken stock, 1/2 gallon water, the potato and the blackened garlic. Mash the potato and the garlic with a whisk and bring to a boil. Reduce to a rapid simmer and cook for about an hour and 15 minutes.

4 Strain out the solids from the soup, and puree them in a blender or food processor, along with enough broth to ease things along. Return the puree to the soup and restore the boil. Add the milk, basil, thyme, salt pepper and Tabasco.

5 Ladle the soup into bowls and garnish with fresh basil. Float a toasted, garlic-buttered slice of French bread on top.

Serves 10.

NUTRITION INFORMATION PER SERVING
96 calories
1 gm. fat
0 gm. saturated fat
110 mg. sodium

Crema Di Funghi Coltivati
Cream of Mushroom Soup

1 Tbs. margarine
1 medium onion, cut up
1 rib celery, chopped
1 leek, well washed, white part only
2 lbs. medium mushrooms, well washed, patted dry and sliced
1 medium potato, peeled and cubed
1 gallon chicken stock
1 cup skimmed evaporated milk
1 cup skim milk
Salt and white pepper, as needed

1   Heat margarine in a large saucepan over medium heat and saute onions, celery, and leeks until onions brown lightly. Add the mushrooms to the saucepan and saute lightly for about a minute.

2   Add the potatoes and chicken stock and heat to a boil. Lower heat and keep soup on a fast simmer for about 25-30 minutes—until potatoes are tender.

3   Remove from fire and strain through a course sieve. Put solid parts strained from soup into a food processor and puree, using 1/4 cup of the soup to help things along if necessary. Return puree to soup.

4 . In a skillet, boil skimmed evaporated milk and milk together and reduce by half. Stir into soup and return to a boil. Adjust seasonings with salt and pepper.

Serves eight.

NUTRITION INFORMATION PER SERVING
80 calories
1 gm. fat
0 gm. saturated fat
95 mg. sodium

Zuppa Di Lenticchie

Lentil Soup

1 lb. lentils
1 Tbs. olive oil
1/2 cup chopped onions
1 rib celery, with leaves, chopped coarsely
1/2 carrot, chopped coarsely
2 Tbs. chopped garlic
1/2 tsp. crushed red pepper
1 cup dry red wine
1/2 cup canned, chopped Italian plum tomatoes
1 gallon beef stock
1/4 tsp. salt
Pinch white pepper
4 sprigs parsley, finely chopped
6 sprigs oregano
1 large bay leaf

Garnish:

Chopped Italian parsley
Grated Parmesan cheese

1   Wash the lentils well and drain.
2   In a skillet, add the oil and heat it to almost smoking temperature. Saute onions, celery, garlic and crushed red pepper until the onions start to brown at the edges. Add the red wine and bring it to a boil.
3   Add lentils, tomatoes and beef stock, and return to a boil. Add the salt, pepper, parsley, oregano, bay leaf and celery leaves. Cover and bring to a boil.
4   Lower heat to a fast simmer for 45 minutes, or until lentils are tender. Remove from the heat.
5   Ladle soup into serving bowls and top with chopped parsley, and grated Parmesan cheese at the table.
Serves eight to ten.

NUTRITIONAL INFORMATION PER SERVING
106 Calories
2 gm. fat
0 gm. of saturated fat
107 mg. sodium

Zuppa Di Pasta E Fagioli
Pasta and White Bean Soup

4 oz. fagioli cannellini (Great Northern beans)
1 Tbs. olive oil
1 oz. boiled ham
1/2 cup chopped onions
1/2 cup chopped carrots
1/4 cup chopped leek, bulb only
2 tsp. chopped garlic
1/2 tsp. crushed red pepper
1/4 cup dry white wine
1/2 cup peeled, seeded, and crushed tomato, with lots of juice
6 cups of chicken stock
3 cups veal stock
Leaves from two ribs of celery
1 1/2 tsp. fresh oregano
1 1/2 tsp. shredded fresh basil
2 cups tubetti or small shell pasta, cooked al dente

1   Sort through beans to pick out the bad ones and foreign matter, and soak beans in water for a minimum of three hours or overnight.

2   In a large saucepan or Dutch oven, cook onions and ham in olive oil over medium heat until onions become tan. Add carrots, leeks, garlic and crushed red pepper and saute until tender.

3   Add beans and wine, and bring to a boil. As soon as bubbles appear add tomato, three cups of the chicken stock, veal stock, celery leaves, oregano and basil. Let soup simmer slowly for at least two hours, stirring occasionally.

4   Add the rest of the chicken stock and three cups of water as needed to keep the soup liquid. Skim excess fat from top of soup. You will find that the soup will very quickly begin throwing off a superlative aroma that will make you very hungry. When the beans in the soup begin to get tender, cook the pasta, drain it, and add it to the soup.

5   Stir well and serve with grated Parmesan cheese.
Serves eight.

NUTRITION INFORMATION PER SERVING
116 calories
2 gm. fat
Less than 1 gm. saturated fat
91 mg. sodium

Minestrone

Italian Vegetable Soup

1 cup dried red beans
1 Tbs. olive oil
1 cup chopped onion
1 Tbs. chopped garlic
1 cup chopped carrots
1 cup chopped celery
1 leek, white part only, washed well, chopped
2 Tbs. tomato paste
2 quarts chicken or beef stock (we use a combination of both)
2 bay leaves
1 large white potato, peeled and diced
1 large zucchini, chopped coarsely
4 oz. green beans
1/4 tsp. salt
1/4 tsp. white pepper
1/4 lb. fresh spinach, washed and large stems removed
5 cloves garlic, peeled
1/2 cup Italian parsley leaves
8 fresh basil leaves
1 stem fresh oregano leaves
2 cups tubetti pasta, cooked al dente

1   Pick through the red beans to remove bad ones. Soak in cold water for
several hours. Drain the water.
2   Boil the beans for one hour in one gallon of fresh water. Pour off water
and reserve beans.
3   In a large saucepan over medium heat, add the oil and get it hot.
Saute onions, garlic, carrots and celery until onions turn blond. Add leeks
and tomato paste and saute for about a minute.
4   Add stocks and bring to a boil. Add bay leaves and red beans, and
continue to simmer for about 30 minutes. Then add the potato and zucchini
and return to a simmer.
5   Meanwhile, bring two quarts of water to a boil in a saucepan. Add
green beans and boil for five minutes. Remove green beans and wash with
cold water. In the same boiling water, poach the spinach for about 45
seconds, and then wash it with cold water. Cut beans and chop spinach and
add to soup pot. Add salt and pepper.
6   In the bowl of a food processor, combine garlic, parsley, basil and
oregano. Puree this.
7   When potatoes in soup are tender, add cooked pasta. Stir in and serve
immediately with grated Parmesan cheese and the herb puree on top.
   Serves eight.

NUTRITION INFORMATION PER SERVING
150 calories
2 gm. fat
0 gm. saturated fat
450 mg. sodium

Stracciatella Di Medici

Spinach and Egg Soup

1 quart beef stock
1 quart chicken stock
1/2 lb. fresh spinach, washed and stems removed
1 Tbs. chopped Italian parsley
2 whole eggs
2 additional egg whites
1/2 cup grated Parmesan cheese
Pinch salt and pepper

1   Mix stocks and bring to a simmer in a large saucepan.
2   Bring about two cups of water to a light boil in a second saucepan. Poach the spinach for about 45 seconds. Remove, chop coarsely, and mix with parsley. Add that mixture to hot stock.
3   Beat the eggs in a bowl. Stir the Parmesan cheese into the eggs. Add egg-and-cheese mixture to stock and stir lightly, until egg and cheese are evenly distributed. Do not stir more than about 15 seconds.
4   Let soup return to a simmer. Stir soup again with kitchen fork to break up eggs, which will have congealed somewhat at top. Add salt and pepper to taste.

Serve hot with grated Parmesan cheese at the table.
Serves eight.

NUTRITION INFORMATION PER SERVING
65 calories
3 gm. fat
1 gm. saturated fat
220 mg. sodium

Zuppa Di Fave

Fava Bean Soup

1 lb. fava beans
1 Tbs. olive oil
1 cup chopped onions
1 Tbs. chopped garlic
1/2 tsp. red crushed pepper
1 oz. boiled ham, chopped
2 quarts chicken stock
2 medium white potatoes, peeled and diced
1 tsp. chopped Italian parsley
1 tsp. chopped celery leaves
2 shallots, peeled and chopped
1/2 tsp. salt
1/4 tsp. white pepper

1 Soak fava beans in water overnight and remove the tough outer skins.

2 In a large saucepan, heat olive oil over medium heat. Saute onions, garlic, crushed red pepper and ham until onions turn light brown.

3 Add beans and saute them about 10 minutes over low flame. Add chicken stock. Bring the pot to a boil, then lower heat and simmer for about two hours.

4 When fava beans are tender, add potatoes, parsley, celery leaves, shallots, salt and pepper. Continue to simmer until potatoes are tender (about 15-20 minutes).

Pasta can also be added to this dish if you like. Serve with a teaspoon of Parmesan cheese at the table.

Serves eight.

NUTRITION INFORMATION PER SERVING
115 calories
3 gm. fat
Less than 1 gm. saturated fat
306 mg. sodium

Crema D'Asparagi

Asparagus Soup

1 medium-large potato, peeled and chopped into cubes
1 Tbs. olive oil
1 rib celery, chopped
1 leek, well washed and chopped
1 medium onion, chopped
2 lbs. asparagus stem bottoms
1 cup white wine
2 quarts beef or chicken stock (we use a combination of the two)
2 cups skim evaporated milk
Salt and pepper to taste
8 tender asparagus tips

1   Saute potatoes briefly in olive oil then add celery, leeks, onions and saute until onions turn a translucent blond.

2   Add asparagus and white wine and bring to a boil briefly. Add stock and return to a boil. Reduce heat and simmer the soup until asparagus becomes tender (about an hour and a half).

3   Meanwhile, heat a small saucepan of water to a boil and poach the asparagus tips for four minutes until just tender. Remove, wash with cold water, and reserve.

4   Strain soup. Put the solid parts in a food processor and puree. (This may take a few minutes, given the woody, stringy quality of asparagus). Add the puree back to the soup, and return soup to a boil.

5   After 10 minutes of simmering, strain the soup through a sieve. Discard the solid parts and return soup to a simmer.

6   In a skillet, bring skimmed evaporated milk to a boil and reduce by one quarter. Whisk the milk into the soup.

7   Add salt and pepper to taste. Ladle soup into bowls, and top each bowl with one asparagus tip.
   Serves eight.

NUTRITION INFORMATION PER SERVING
125 calories
1 gm. fat
0 gm. saturated fat
138 mg. sodium

Zuppa Di Broccoli
Broccoli Soup

1 Tbs. olive oil
2 ribs celery
1 medium onion, cut into chunks
1/2 Tbs. chopped garlic
8-10 broccoli stems, cut into chunks
1 medium large potato, trimmed and cut into chunks
2 quarts beef or chicken stock, or a combination of the two
2 bay leaves
1/8 tsp. salt
Pinch white pepper
Florets from one stalk of broccoli
1 cup skimmed evaporated milk

1   Heat the olive oil in a saucepan under medium-high heat and saute the celery, onion, and garlic until vegetables turn blond.

2   Add broccoli stems and potato to saucepan, and follow immediately with stock, bay leaf, salt and pepper. Bring to a boil and cook until broccoli stems are tender (about two hours).

3   Meanwhile, boil two cups of water in a saucepan. Break the broccoli florets into three pieces and boil for five minutes until tender at the outside but still firm. Break into small pieces and reserve.

4   Strain soup. Puree remaining solid parts in a food processor. Return puree to soup pot, and return pot to stove. When soup returns to a boil, strain through a sieve. Stir in milk and simmer for five or 10 more minutes.

5   Ladle soup into bowls and top with a few of the reserved florets.
Serves eight.

NUTRITION INFORMATION PER SERVING
75 calories
2 gm. fat
0 gm. saturated fat
90 mg. sodium

Gumbo Di Frutti Di Mare
Seafood Gumbo

1 lb. crab shells, legs, and claws, pulled apart
1/4 tsp. dried thyme
3 bay leaves
2 cups all-purpose flour
1 Tbs. olive oil
1/2 cup chopped onions
1 Tbs. chopped garlic
1/4 leek, chopped
1 medium green bell pepper, chopped
2 ribs celery, chopped
1 tsp. crushed red pepper
1 lb. fresh okra
4 Italian plum tomatoes, broken up with the fingers
1 cup uncooked rice
1/4 cup claw crabmeat
1 cup lump crabmeat, well-picked to remove shells
12 oz. small chopped shrimp
16-24 oysters, depending on size, cut large ones in half
1/4 tsp. cayenne
1/2 tsp. salt
1 tsp. white pepper
1 tsp. black pepper
1 tsp. Tabasco
1 Tbs. Worcestershire

Preheat oven to 400 degrees.

1 In a covered saucepan, boil a gallon of cold water with the crab shells, claws, and legs for 30 minutes until you get a good crab flavor in the stock. Add the thyme and bay leaves, and continue to boil for another few minutes.

2 Meanwhile, make a roux. This roux is made with absolutely no oil. In the preheated oven, heat a large cast iron skillet until it is quite hot. Sprinkle the flour on the bottom and return to the oven. Check the flour every couple of minutes as it browns, stirring it thoroughly now and then. When it's the color of walnuts, remove the skillet from the oven.

3 In a second skillet, saute the onions, garlic, leeks, green peppers, celery and crushed red pepper in olive oil until tender. Slowly add the browned flour to the sauteed vegetables and stir well.

4 Add the crab stock, shells and all, to the mixture. Return to a light boil over medium heat, whisking the ingredients well.

5 Cut off the stem ends of the okra, then slice the rest about 1/4 inch thick. Once the gumbo has been boiling for 20 minutes, add the okra and the tomatoes.

6 Bring one quart of cold water to a boil and add the rice. Boil for five minutes until cooked but still firm. Wash the rice with cold water to stop cooking, and set aside.

7 After the gumbo has boiled another 20 minutes add the crabmeat, shrimp, and oysters. Boil for another three minutes then add the cayenne, salt, black and white peppers, Tabasco and Worcestershire. Adjust seasonings to taste.

8 To serve, put about two Tbs. cooked rice on each soup plate, and ladle gumbo over it.

Serves 12.

NUTRITION INFORMATION PER SERVING
228 calories
2 gm. fat
0 gm. saturated fat
365 mg. sodium

Zuppa Di Pollo Dannon
Chicken Yogurt Soup

1 Tbs. margarine
7 oz. whole chicken breast, bones and skin removed
1/2 medium onion, chopped
1 stalk celery, chopped
1 clove garlic, pressed or crushed
1 small potato, peeled and cubed
1 cup white wine
2 bay leaves
2 sprigs fresh thyme, chopped
8 oz. plain low-fat yogurt
Salt and pepper

1 Heat margarine in a skillet over medium high heat. Saute the chicken, onion, celery, and garlic until lightly browned.

2 Add potato, wine, 1/2 cup water, and bay leaves. Simmer for 20 minutes.

3 Remove chicken and dice. Discard the bay leaf.

4 Place the remaining liquid in blender and puree. Strain and allow to cool. Add thyme, yogurt, salt and pepper to taste. Add chicken and chill.

5 Serve in chilled bowls. Garnish with fresh chopped green onion.
Makes five one-cup servings.

NUTRITION INFORMATION PER SERVING
154 calories
3 gm. fat
1 gm. saturated fat
129 mg. sodium

Crema Di Pomodori

Tomato Bisque

2 lbs. fresh ripe tomatoes
1 Tbs. olive oil
1 cup chopped onion
2 ribs celery, coarsely chopped
1/2 leek, well washed and coarsely chopped
1 cup carrot, peeled and sliced
1 Tbs. chopped garlic
4 Tbs. tomato paste
1/4 tsp. crushed red pepper
1 cup dry white wine
1 cup dry vermouth
1/2 gallon beef stock
1/2 cup fresh basil, chopped
1 cup uncooked rice (Uncle Ben's)
1 cup skimmed evaporated milk
8 leaves fresh basil, cut into thin strips
1/4 tsp. salt
1/4 tsp. white pepper

1   Preheat oven to 400 degrees.

2   Cut the tomatoes in half, cut out the stem cores, and squeeze out the seeds. Reserve two tomatoes; chop the rest coarsely.

3   In a large saucepan, heat the olive oil over low heat. Saute the onion, celery, leek, carrot and garlic until moist and tender. Stir in the tomato paste and the crushed red pepper.

4   Add the white wine and vermouth and bring to a boil. Reduce liquid by half. Add the beef stock, 1/2 gallon of water, chopped basil and chopped tomatoes. Return to a boil, then lower heat and simmer for 50 minutes.

5   Add the uncooked rice to the pot. Cook another 30 minutes.

6   Put the contents of the pot into a food processor or blender and puree (yes, with the rice in it). You can do this in batches if necessary. Strain the result through a sieve. Discard the solids, of which there may be quite a bit.

7   Return the soup to the saucepan over medium heat. Stir in skimmed evaporated milk, salt, pepper and basil. Bring to a boil.

8   Meanwhile, peel the reserved tomatoes, and slice them into thin half-moons; add them now to the pot. When the tomato slices are warm, remove the soup from the heat and serve.

Serves eight.

NUTRITION INFORMATION PER SERVING
175 calories
2 gm. fat
0 gm. saturated fat
161 mg. sodium

Pasta

Homemade Semolina Pasta

Pasta is one of the world's greatest foods. It is very healthful, being low in fat and high in complex carbohydrates. It is delicious and, best of all, endlessly adaptable. You can make pasta in any imaginable shape and serve it with almost any food.

I highly recommend that you invest in a small pasta machine for your kitchen and make your own fresh pasta. It is no more difficult than making any other kind of dough and it gives superior results. Although there are many complicated pasta machines on the market, the best gadget for making pasta is hand-operated and very simple.

A good pasta maker will be made of stainless steel. It is not cheap, but it pays off in long life and better pasta. It consists of a set of gear-driven rollers, about six inches long. By varying the space between the rollers, you control the thickness of the pasta.

Regardless of what shape you make your pasta, here is the formula for making the dough.

2 cups semolina flour
2 cups all-purpose flour
2 eggs, well beaten
1 Tbs. extra virgin olive oil
1/2 tsp. salt

1   Mix the two flours together and make a mound on top of a clean surface. Make a well in the center of the mound.

2   In a large bowl, beat the eggs and mix in the olive oil, salt and one cup cold water. Pour this into the flour well.

3   With your hands, mix the flours and liquids together and knead until you have a ball of dough. Add up to another 1/2 cup of water to help things along, as necessary. Work the dough by rolling it away from you on the counter while simultaneously tearing it in half. Then pull it back together while rolling it back towards you, always keeping some pressure on the dough with the balls of your hands. Keep rolling and tearing for five minutes, until the mixture is uniform and smooth. Dust with flour now and then to keep the dough from sticking.

4   Make the dough into the shape of a bread loaf and dust with white flour. Cover with a dry cloth and allow the pasta dough ball to rest for five minutes. Cut off a piece of dough about the size of your fist and flatten it into a disk. Dust it lightly with flour.

The dough is now ready to be shaped using your pasta machine.
Makes 1 1/2 pounds of fresh pasta.

NUTRITION INFORMATION PER SERVING
(2-oz. portion)
175 calories
2 gm. fat
0 gm. saturated fat
94 mg. sodium

Linguine Bolognese
Linguine with Meat Sauce

28 oz. beef tenderloin tips, trimmed of fat
1 rib celery, chopped
1/2 medium onion, chopped
1 medium carrot, chopped
1/2 Tbsp. chopped garlic
1/4 tsp. chopped fresh rosemary
1 Tbsp. tomato paste
1/2 cup dry red wine
1 Tbsp. all-purpose flour
1 quart beef stock
3 bay leaves
1/3 tsp. white pepper
4 canned Italian plum tomatoes, chopped, with plenty of juice (no added salt)
1/2 tsp. fresh sage, chopped
1 lb. linguine, fettuccine, mostaccioli, or other pasta
8 Tbsp. part-skim Parmesan cheese

1   Chop the beef into small morsels; you may also use a meat grinder, but keep the meat coarse.
2   Spray skillet with olive oil. Saute the ground beef, stirring constantly, until uniformly browned.
3   Stir in the chopped vegetables and continue cooking until vegetables are tender and mixture is dry. Stir occasionally.
4   Stir in the chopped garlic, rosemary, and the tomato paste. Cook for a minute or two, then pour in the red wine and bring to a boil. Sprinkle in the flour and stir well. Add the beef stock, bay leaves, and bring to a boil.
5   Stir in the tomatoes and juice and return to a boil. Lower the heat to a simmer. Add the sage, and simmer the pot for an hour and 15 minutes.
6   Cook the pasta al dente and drain. Put the pasta into bowls and serve the sauce on top. Sprinkle 1 Tbsp. grated part-skim Parmesan cheese on each serving.
    Serves eight.

NUTRITIONAL INFORMATION PER SERVING
340 Calories
11.5 gm. fat
89 mg. cholesterol
455 mg. sodium

Pasta Aglio Olio

Pasta With Garlic And Olive Oil

3 Tbs. extra virgin olive oil
1 Tbs. chopped garlic
1 Tbs. chopped onion
1/4 tsp. crushed red pepper
2 Tbs. chopped fresh Italian parsley
1/4 tsp. salt
Pinch white pepper
8 oz. fresh pasta, cooked al dente

1   In a skillet, heat the olive oil over medium heat. Saute the onions and garlic until translucent.

2   Add the crushed red pepper, parsley, salt, and pepper. Cook for about a minute more, then add 1/2 cup of the water in which the pasta was boiled. Whisk the skillet to blend the sauce thoroughly.

3   Lower the heat and add the cooked pasta to the skillet and toss with the sauce until the sauce is well distributed. Serve with Parmesan cheese.
Serves four.

NUTRITION INFORMATION PER SERVING
2 oz. portion
275 calories
12 gm. fat
1 gm. saturated fat
197 mg. sodium

Lasagna "Nello"
Lasagna with Meat and Cheese

1/2 lb. ground inside round
1-1/2 Tbsp. chopped garlic
1/4 cup chopped onions
1 Tbsp. chopped fresh oregano
2 Tbsp. chopped Italian parsley
1 Tbsp. chopped fresh basil
1/4 tsp. white pepper
1/4 cup grated part-skim Parmesan cheese
1/4 cup bread crumbs
8 sheets pasta dough, 6 inches by 18 inches
2 quarts tomato basil sauce
1 lb. spinach, well washed and coarse stem removed
2 cups shredded part-skim Mozzarella cheese
1-1/2 cups part-skim Ricotta cheese
1/2 cup grated part-skim Parmesan cheese

Preheat oven to 400 degrees.

1   Combine ground meat, garlic, onions, oregano, parsley, basil, parmesan cheese and bread crumbs in a mixer or food processor. Scoop out irregular one-teaspoon meatballs and place them, well apart from one another, on a baking sheet. Bake the meatballs for five minutes at 400 degrees. Remove and reserve.

2   Cook the pasta sheets, four at a time, in two gallons of boiling water about 4 minutes. Boil without added salt or oil. Take the pasta out and wash it with cold water. Set aside to drain.

3   Poach spinach for two minutes in boiling water, then chop very fine in a food processor.

4   Spray the bottom of the baking pan (or pans) with olive oil, then cover it with a layer of pasta - two sheets lengthwise across the pan. Pour two cups of tomato basil sauce over the pasta and spread it out.

5   Intersperse about a third of the meatballs, 1/3 cup of part-skim ricotta cheese, 1/2 cup mozzarella, and 1/4 cup of the chopped spinach for the next layer.

6   Lay down, at right angles to the sheets of pasta in the first layer, another layer of pasta. Top this with another layer of sauce, meatballs. cheeses and spinach as before.

7   Repeat step 6. Then another layer of pasta, topped with 2 cups of sauce and the remaining mozzarella and parmesan cheeses.

8   Place the entire pan inside another pan of the same size filled about one-third full with water. Put the entire double pan inside a preheated 450-degree oven and bake for 30 minutes. Lower the heat to 350 degrees and continue baking for another ten minutes.

9 After taking it out the oven, allow the lasagna to cool for 15 minutes before attempting to serve it. Slice it into twelve pieces, and serve with 4 oz. of tomato basil sauce.
Serves twelve

NUTRITIONAL INFORMATION PER SERVING
299 Calories
8 gm. fat
33 gm. of cholesterol
449 mg. sodium

Salsa Pomidoro Basilico
Tomato Basil Sauce

1 Tbs. olive oil
1/8 cup chopped onion
1 tsp. chopped garlic
1/4 cup red wine
2 cups canned Italian plum tomatoes
2 cups juice from tomatoes
1/2 tsp. salt
1/4 tsp. white pepper
2 sprigs chopped fresh oregano
8 chopped fresh basil leaves
4 chopped sprigs of Italian parsley
1 bay leaf

1 In a saucepan over medium heat, heat the olive oil until very hot. In it saute the onions and garlic until they turn blond. Add wine and bring to a boil.

2 Immediately add the tomatoes, squeezing them between your fingers to break them up as you add them. Add tomato juice. Lower the heat and simmer the sauce.

3 After about 30 minutes, add water (a cup or less) if necessary to give the sauce the right consistency. You want the sauce thin enough to be able to easily coat pasta, yet not so thin that it runs off the pasta. Add salt, pepper, oregano, basil, parsley and bay leaf.

4 Simmer sauce another 15-20 minutes. Adjust seasonings as needed.
Makes about one quart. Enough for about 8 pasta entrees.

NUTRITION INFORMATION PER SERVING
(Two-ounce serving)
36 calories
0 gm. fat
0 gm. saturated fat
220 mg. sodium

Salsa Pesto
Pesto Sauce

2 cups fresh basil leaves, loosely packed
1/4 cup chopped onion
2 Tbs. chopped garlic
1/2 cup extra virgin olive oil
2 Tbs. grated Parmesan cheese
2 Tbs. toasted pine nuts
1/2 tsp. salt
1/4 tsp. white pepper

1   Pick through basil and remove large stems and bad leaves. Chop basil fine in a food processor. Add onions and garlic to the processor bowl and puree. Set aside in a large bowl.

2   Put one stick of margarine into the processor and give it a whirl. Add half of the olive oil, followed by another stick of margarine, followed by the other half of the olive oil, blending well as you go until you have a thick liquid. Pour margarine-oil mixture into a bowl with the basil puree. Add Parmesan cheese, pine nuts, salt and pepper. Stir well until completely blended.

This will make about three cups of sauce. It can be kept for a long time in the refrigerator if tightly sealed.

PASTA WITH PESTO

1   Cook 1 lb. (dry weight) of your favorite pasta in salted water until al dente. Drain well.

2   Warm a large skillet over medium heat. Put the pasta into the skillet and spoon 4 Tbs. of pesto sauce over the pasta. With a kitchen fork, toss and blend with the pasta. The sauce will break if you put it into the skillet first—always stir the sauce into the pasta rather than vice-versa.

Serves six.

NUTRITION INFORMATION PER SERVING
392 calories
21 gm. fat
3 gm. saturated fat
203 mg. sodium

Canneloni Andrea
Pasta Tubes with Meat Stuffing

2 Tbs. extra virgin olive oil
3 oz. ground lean beef
3 oz. ground white veal
2 Tbs. chopped onion
1 tsp. chopped garlic
1 Tbs. chopped carrot
1 Tbs. chopped celery
1 Tbs. tomato paste
1/4 cup dry red wine
12 sheets fresh pasta, 4" square
2 oz. part-skim mozzarella cheese
1 oz. low-fat ricotta cheese
1 oz. Parmesan cheese
1 egg
Pinch nutmeg
Pinch chopped rosemary
Pinch sage
12 oz. tomato basil sauce, strained (see sauces)

Preheat the oven to 350 degrees.

1   Heat the olive oil in a skillet and in it cook the ground beef and veal, stirring well until it is lightly browned throughout.

2   Add the onions, garlic, carrots and celery and cook over medium-low heat until the vegetables are moist.

3   Stir in the tomato paste and the wine. Bring the mixture to a boil and reduce the liquid by about half. Remove the skillet from the heat and allow the mixture to cool.

4   Meanwhile, cook the pasta al dente. Drain the sheets well and spread them out on a sheet of waxed paper.

5   When the stuffing is lukewarm, stir in the cheeses and herbs. Then stir in the egg. The best way to do this is with your fingers. Don't use a food processor, as it will pulverize the meat too much.

6   When the mixture is uniform in texture, put it into a pastry bag with a broad tip and pipe about two ounces along one short edge of the pasta sheets. Roll up the sheets carefully to form tubes. Place the tubes, close but not touching, into a baking pan coated lightly with olive oil. Put two Tbs. of water into the pan.

7   Cover the pan with aluminum foil and bake in a preheated 350-degree oven for 15 minutes.

8   Allow the cannelloni to cool for five minutes. Remove with a spatula and serve two per person. Nap with 4 oz. tomato basil sauce, parsley and grated Parmesan cheese.

Serves six.

NUTRITION INFORMATION PER SERVING
242 calories
9 gm. fat
4 gm. saturated fat
323 mg. sodium

Paglia e Fieno

"Hay And Straw" Pasta With Beef Tips

1/2 Tbs. extra virgin olive oil
1/2 tsp. chopped garlic
1 Tbs. chopped onion
4 oz. tenderloin beef, cubed
2 whole mushrooms, sliced
1/2 Tbs. fresh parsley
1/2 Tbs. fresh oregano
1/8 tsp. crushed red pepper
1/3 cup red wine
1/3 cup tomato sauce
1/4 cup skimmed evaporated milk
2 sun-dried tomatoes, sliced in strips
4 leaves fresh basil, chopped
4 oz. green and white fettuccine, cooked al dente

1 In a skillet over medium heat, saute garlic and onion in olive oil until tender. Add the beef and mushrooms, and saute for 2-3 minutes. Add herbs and spices and continue to stir for two more minutes.

2 Add red wine, tomato sauce and skimmed evaporated milk, sun-dried tomatoes and fresh basil. Cook down for approximately five minutes.

3 Serve over 4 oz. green and white fettuccine, cooked al dente. May add Parmesan cheese if desired.
Serves two.

NUTRITION INFORMATION PER SERVING
(without Parmesan cheese)
183 calories
5 gm. fat
1 gm. saturated fat
50 mg. sodium

Ravioli Con Granchio

Crabmeat Ravioli

1 Tbs. margarine
1 Tbs. extra virgin olive oil
3 Tbs. chopped onions
1 Tbs. chopped garlic
1 lb. lump crabmeat
2 leaves fresh sage, chopped
3 sprigs Italian parsley, chopped
1/2 tsp. dried marjoram
1 tsp. salt
1/4 tsp. white pepper
Pinch cayenne
Pinch nutmeg
2 Tbs. brandy
1/4 dry white wine
1 Tbs. Worcestershire
1/4 cup bread crumbs
1/4 cup Parmesan cheese
12 sheets fresh pasta, about 3 inches by 9 inches each
1 beaten egg

Sauce:
2 tsp. margarine
2 tsp. chopped garlic
1/4 cup dry white wine
1 quart fish stock
1 quart skimmed evaporated milk
1/4 cup Parmesan cheese
1 tsp. salt
1/4 tsp. white pepper

1 Heat the margarine and olive oil in a skillet over medium heat and saute the onions and garlic until translucent. Add the crabmeat and heat through—about one minute. Add the sage, parsley, marjoram, salt, pepper, cayenne and nutmeg.

2 Add the brandy and flame it carefully. Add the white wine and Worcestershire and bring to a boil. When all liquid is absorbed or evaporated, remove contents of skillet to a cool pan.

3 While waiting for the crabmeat stuffing to cool, make the sauce. Melt butter in a saucepan and saute garlic for about a minute. Add white wine and cream to skillet and bring cream to a boil. After two minutes add the fish stock and return to a boil. Reduce by half, then whisk in Parmesan cheese, salt and pepper. Remove from heat but keep warm.

4 When the crabmeat mixture is cool, add the bread crumbs and Parmesan cheese. Process the mixture in a food processor into a rough mixture—with some noticeable pieces of crabmeat remaining.

5 To stuff the ravioli, you will need a ravioli form, available at cookware shops. Place a sheet of pasta over the metal part of the form (the part with the holes in it). Make depressions in the pasta by pushing down with the plastic mold that comes with the form. Brush the pasta with beaten egg.

6 Fill each depression with about a teaspoon of the crabmeat stuffing.

7 Place another sheet of pasta over the stuffing. Use the plastic mold upside down to push the two pieces of pasta together firmly. Use a knife to cut the individual ravioli apart.

8 Cook the ravioli is a pot of boiling salted water for about six minutes. Remove and drain well.

9 Return the skillet with the sauce to medium heat until it begins to bubble. Add a few well-drained ravioli (just enough to cover the bottom of the pan, without overlapping each other) and cook until the ravioli are warmed through and have been sloshed around in the sauce. Immediately remove from heat and serve. Repeat until all ravioli are warmed and sauced.

Makes 60 ravioli—about eight entrees or 16 appetizers.

NUTRITION INFORMATION PER SERVING
272 calories
9 gm. fat
1 gm. saturated fat
750 mg. sodium

Fettuccine Alfredo
Noodles with Cream and Egg

1 Tbs. margarine
2 Tbs. chopped onion
1 tsp. chopped garlic
1/2 cup dry white wine
12 oz. (1 can) skimmed evaporated milk
Pinch nutmeg
1/2 tsp, salt
Pinch white pepper
1 egg yolk
8 oz. fettuccine, cooked al dente

1 In a skillet over medium heat, heat the margarine until it bubbles. In it saute the onions and garlic until they turn translucent. Add wine and bring to a light boil until reduced by half. Add evaporated milk and half-and half. Reduce down to about two-thirds original volume.

2 Strain the sauce through a sieve. Return to the skillet over medium heat and simmer. Add nutmeg, salt and pepper. Whisk in the egg yolk thoroughly.

3 Drain the fettuccine well. Add it to the skillet with the sauce. Toss to coat the pasta completely with the sauce. Serve with freshly cracked black pepper and grated Parmesan cheese at the table.

Serves four.

NUTRITION INFORMATION PER SERVING
200 calories
3 gm. fat
1 gm. saturated fat
423 mg. sodium

Cappelli D'Angelo Andrea
Angel Hair Pasta With Smoked Salmon

1 Tbs. margarine
1/4 cup chopped onion
1 tsp. chopped garlic
3 oz. smoked salmon, sliced into strips
1/2 cup 100-proof vodka
1/2 cup dry white wine
1 cup fish stock
12 oz. skimmed evaporated milk
Salt and white pepper to taste
12 oz. angel hair pasta (cappellini), cooked al dente
2 tsp. black caviar
2 sprigs fresh snipped dill (optional)

1 In a skillet over medium heat, heat the margarine until it bubbles. In it saute the onions and garlic until they turn translucent. Add salmon and saute until the color changes to a pale orange.

2 Pour in the vodka and carefully flame it. When flames die out, remove pan contents and keep warm.

3 Without cleaning the pan, add the wine and fish stock and bring to a boil. Add the evaporated milk and reduce the sauce over medium-low heat by about half. Add salmon mixture and return to a simmer. Taste sauce, then add salt and pepper. (Smoked salmon sometimes carries a lot of salt, enough to affect the salt content of the whole dish.)

4 Meanwhile, cook the pasta al dente. Remember that angel hair cooks very quickly—a minute or two is enough for fresh, four minutes for dried. Drain the pasta well, but save one cup of the water.

5 Add pasta to the skillet of sauce with two Tbs. of the pasta water. Toss briefly over low heat to coat pasta well with sauce. Serve the pasta with lots of sauce. Garnish with one of the salmon strips, 1/2 tsp. of caviar, and fresh dill.

Serves two entrees or four appetizers.

NUTRITION INFORMATION PER SERVING
270 calories
5 gm. fat
1 gm. saturated fat
272 mg. sodium

Gnocchi Regina
Potato Pasta Dumplings

3 lbs. white Idaho potatoes
1/4 cup margarine
2 egg yolks
13 oz. all-purpose flour
1/4 tsp. nutmeg

1   Scrub potatoes in cold water. Boil for an hour to 90 minutes, depending on the size of the potatoes. Here's how to tell when the potatoes are cooked: Put the blade of a kitchen knife through the center of the potato while it's still in the pot, and pull the knife up. If the knife slides out, the potato is done. If it picks the potato up out of the water, it's not done.

2   When cooked, remove potatoes from the water. While still hot, peel and slice the potatoes, and run them through a food mill to mash smooth with no lumps.

3   Melt the margarine in a deep skillet or saucepan over low heat. Add the mashed potatoes and stir vigorously to mix. This will create a very stiff mixture, almost like bread dough.

4   Stir egg yolks, one at a time, into the potato mixture. Do this quickly before yolks have a chance to cook from the heat of the potatoes, and keep stirring. When eggs are incorporated completely into potatoes, remove from stove.

5   Scoop the potato "dough" on top of a clean smooth surface, dusted with flour. Add flour about 1/2 cup at a time, and knead it into the potatoes. Sprinkle a little extra flour over the potato dough and counter if necessary to prevent sticking.

6   Cut off about a fifth of the dough. Roll it out to a long, thin (about 1/2-inch diameter) "snake." With a flour-dusted knife, cut off pieces of the "snake" about 1/2 inch long.

7   With your thumb, roll each piece of dough along the tines of a table fork. As you do this, press down so the dough curls in on itself a little. This will result in a nugget with a large indentation on one side and ridges across the other—the classic gnocchi shape. This is very time consuming, but it's a therapeutic, calming activity for one, or a nice conversational backdrop for two.

8   Put the gnocchi on a floured pan in one well-spaced layer. This recipe makes about 300 gnocchi—enough for 12 servings. You can preserve it for later use. Allow the gnocchi to dry for about two hours in the pan. Then place them in plastic bags and freeze.

9   When you're ready to use the gnocchi, put them right into boiling water. (Even if they're frozen. They do not need to be defrosted first.) Cook the gnocchi exactly as you would pasta. Boil them for about four minutes (longer if frozen). Drain them and toss them in a skillet with tomato sauce, pesto sauce or your own favorite sauce.

Serves 12.

NUTRITION INFORMATION PER SERVING
240 calories
3 gm. fat
1 gm. saturated fat
35 mg. sodium

Lasagna Di Legume Vegitaria

Vegetable Lasagna

2 lbs. fresh spinach, well washed and coarse stems removed
1 Tbs. extra virgin olive oil
1 lb. zucchini
1 medium eggplant
24 medium mushrooms
3 medium carrots
1 lb. green beans
1 lb. fresh asparagus
1 leek, well washed
1 medium onion, sliced
2 red bell peppers
2 green bell peppers
8 sheets pasta, about 6 by 18 inches
1 1/2 quarts Italian tomato basil sauce (see page 00)
1 cup sun-dried tomatoes, julienne sliced
6 oz. grated fresh Parmesan cheese

1 Wash all the vegetables well. You will need to cook most of them, and each one needs to be cooked a different way. Here goes:

Spinach. Poach for two minutes in boiling water. Try not to break the leaves. When cooked, plunge into cold water to stop the cooking.

Zucchini, eggplant, and mushrooms. Slice lengthwise to the thickness of two stacked quarters. Heat the olive oil in a skillet and saute for two minutes on each side. Drain and keep warm.

Carrots and green beans. Slice carrots diagonally to the thickness of two quarters. Poach in boiling water for five minutes then wash with cold water.

Asparagus. Peel woody skin and poach for six minutes until slightly soft but still firm. Chop into 1/4 in. segments.

Leek. Slice in half from top to bottom. Discard the outer tough leaves and poach the inner sections two minutes. Slice about two in. long.

Onions. Slice about the thickness of two quarters and saute in one Tbs. olive oil until light brown.

Bell peppers. Roast over open fire or under broiler until skin is blackened and blistered all over. Peel skin off. Remove stem, seeds, and membranes. Slice about 1/2 inch wide, two inches long.

Preheat oven to 450 degrees.

2 Bring a large saucepan of water to a boil with about 1/2 tsp. salt. Add the pasta sheets and cook about three minutes for fresh pasta (six to eight minutes if dried). Remove, rinse with cold water and drain.

3 Brush two 9x12x2-inch pans with 1 Tbs. olive oil (total). Cover the pan bottoms with slightly overlapping sheets of pasta.

4 Pour a cup of the tomato-basil sauce in each pan. then stack up the layers in the following order:

Eggplant
Red bell pepper
Pasta (arrange sheets at right angles to the first pasta layer)
1 cup tomato basil sauce per pan
Spinach (spread leaves out flat)
Carrots
Zucchini
Pasta (at right angles to the previous layer)
Sun-dried tomatoes
Mushrooms
Leeks
1 cup tomato basil sauce per pan
1/2 cup Parmesan cheese per pan

5 Put the lasagna pan inside a bigger pan with enough water to come halfway up the sides of the lasagna pan. Bake at 450 degrees for 45 minutes.

6 Remove the lasagna and allow to cool on the top of the stove for 15-30 minutes. Slice into portions of your choice (about six per pan.) Serve with hot tomato basil sauce and Parmesan cheese.

Serves twelve.

NUTRITIONAL INFORMATION PER SERVING
320 Calories
12 gm. fat
3 gm. of saturated fat
143 mg. sodium

Risotto

Basic Recipe

2 qts. chicken stock
1 Tbs. margarine
1 Tbs. chopped onion
1/2 Tbs. chopped garlic
1 lb. Arborio rice
1 cup dry white wine
1/2 tsp. salt
Pinch white pepper

1   Bring the chicken stock to a boil in a large saucepan.

2   Heat the butter in a second saucepan (minimum five-quart capacity) over medium heat. When it begins bubbling, add the onions and garlic and saute until blond.

3   Increase the heat to high and add the rice. Stir well with a kitchen fork (never stir rice with a spoon!) to coat all the rice with the hot butter. When you see the first hint of browning, stir in the wine and lower the heat.

4   Pour in the boiling chicken stock and add the salt and pepper. When the saucepan returns to a boil, put it into a preheated 450-degree oven for 15 to 20 minutes. The rice should have absorbed all but some small wells of unabsorbed, bubbling liquid when you remove it from the oven.

5   Remove the risotto from the saucepan immediately. Spread it out in a large skillet, a pizza pan, or a sheet pan, and allow it to cool. Do not let it cool in the saucepan, as it will continue to cook from its own heat.

Serves six.

NUTRITION INFORMATION PER SERVING
310 calories
1 gm. fat
0 gm. saturated fat
220 mg. sodium

Risotto Pescatore

Seafood Risotto

1 Tbs. extra virgin olive oil
1 Tbs. chopped onion
1 tsp. chopped garlic
1/2 tsp. crushed red pepper
4 fresh mussels in shells, washed well
4 clams in shells, washed well
1/4 cup dry white wine
1 cup chopped canned Italian plum tomatoes, with juice
1 cup fish stock
2 medium squid, cleaned and sliced
4 oysters
4 shrimp, peeled and deveined
4 one-ounce pieces of whote fish (trout, etc.)
4 sea scallops
1 tsp. chopped fresh Italian parsley
1/2 tsp. chopped fresh oregano leaves
2 cups basic risotto (see previous recipe)
Pinch white pepper

1   In a skillet, heat the olive oil over medium heat. Saute the onions, garlic and crushed red pepper until onions are blond.

2   Add mussels and clams and cook, agitating the pan. As they open, remove them to a bowl of warm salted water. Clean out the sand inside the shells. Drain the water and set shellfish aside.

3   Add wine, tomatoes and fish stock to the skillet and bring to a boil. Add other seafoods, parsley, and oregano, and return to a boil.

4   When all the seafoods are cooked, stir in the risotto. Return the mussels and clams to the pan and warm through with the sauce. Add pepper to taste.

Serves four.

NUTRITION INFORMATION PER SERVING
327 calories
5 gm. fat
Less than 1 gm. saturated fat
229 mg. sodium

Seafood

Dentice In Umido
Red Snapper Simmered with Wine and Tomatoes

1 Tbs. extra virgin olive oil
2 garlic cloves, lightly crushed to break skin
1 tsp. crushed red pepper flakes
4 red snapper fillets, 4-6 oz. ea.
1 cup dry white wine
1 cup canned Italian plum tomatoes, chopped
2 cup fish stock
1/4 tsp. salt
Pinch white pepper
3 sprigs fresh oregano leaves

Preheat oven to 400 degrees.

1 Heat olive oil in a skillet over high heat. Saute garlic cloves until they begin to brown around the edges. Add crushed red pepper.

2 Put two fish fillets at a time into the hot skillet, and saute 30 seconds on each side. Remove from pan and keep warm.

3 Add the wine, tomatoes, fish stock, salt, pepper and oregano to the skillet and bring to a boil over high heat. Lower the heat to medium and simmer the sauce for five minutes.

4 Put the fish back in the skillet and put the skillet into the oven for about five minutes until fish is cooked. Nap with the sauce and serve with a sprig of fresh oregano.

Serves four.

NUTRITION INFORMATION PER SERVING
238 calories
6 gm. fat
1 gm. saturated fat
433 mg. sodium

Tonno Con Melanzane
Tuna With Eggplant

1 eggplant
1 tsp. margarine
2 cloves garlic
1 Tbs. chopped onion
1/4 cup fish stock
1/2 cup red wine
1 Tbs. fresh oregano (1/2 tsp. dry)
1 tsp. extra virgin olive oil, divided
4-6 oz. tuna steak

1   Cut the eggplant in half crosswise. Remove the skin from one half and cut into medium dice. Slice the other half about 1/4 inch thick.

2   In a skillet over medium heat, melt the margarine. Add onion, garlic and diced eggplant. Heat for two minutes. Add stock, wine, and herbs. Simmer until liquid evaporates.

3   Remove solid mixture from the skillet and puree in a blender.

4   In a second hot skillet, saute the slices of eggplant in 1/2 tsp. olive oil until tender. Keep warm.

5   Add another 1/2 tsp. olive oil and saute the tuna until medium rare.

6   Reheat the pureed eggplant mixture. On an oven-proof dish, layer a slice of eggplant, then the tuna, then the eggplant mixture. The sauce may also be served on the side.

7   Bake at 450 degrees for five minutes.
Serves four.

NUTRITION INFORMATION PER SERVING
233 calories
3 gm. fat
Less than 1 gm. saturated fat
94 mg. sodium

Tonno alla Fiorentina
Grilled Fresh Tuna with Spinach

1 Tbsp. chopped onions
1/2 Tbsp. chopped garlic
1/2 tsp. crushed red pepper
1/2 tsp. salt
1/4 tsp. pepper
1 lb. fresh spinach, washed well, stems removed
4 sprigs chopped Italian parsley
4 steaks of fresh tuna, 3 oz. each

Sauce:
2 Tbsp. low calorie margarine
1 Tbsp. onion
1 tsp. chopped garlic
1/4 tsp. crushed red pepper
1/4 cup lemon juice
1/4 cup white wine
4 sprigs chopped Italian parsley

1 Spray skillet with olive oil over medium heat and saute the onion, garlic and crushed red pepper until onions are translucent. Add spinach along with one cup water, salt and pepper. Saute until spinach wilts uniformly - about two minutes. (You now have a very good side dish of spinach, although that's not what we're using it for in this recipe.

2 Grill tuna in preheated broiler, on top of a hot barbecue grill, or in a very hot skillet for only about a minute, then turn over and cook another 30 seconds. May spray with olive oil. Careful! Overcooked tuna is like rubber. It should have a slight blush of pink at the center when done.

3 For sauce, heat the low calorie margarine in a skillet. Saute onions, garlic, and crushed red pepper until onions begin to brown around the edges. Add lemon juice, wine and parsley and bring to a very fast boil. When that happens the sauce is finished; remove it from the fire immediately.

4 To serve, spread out the spinach on the plate first. Top it with the tuna steak, and then nap the tuna with 2 Tbsp. of sauce.
Serves four.

NUTRITIONAL INFORMATION PER SERVING
184 Calories
8 gm. fat
32 mg Cholesterol
424 mg. sodium

Cappe Sante e Scampi Valentino

Broiled Shrimp and Scallops on Skewers

8 medium shrimp
8 large scallops
6 slices Canadian bacon
1 Tbsp. chopped onions
1 tsp. chopped garlic
1/8 tsp. crushed red pepper
1 Tbsp. chopped fresh basil leaves
1 Tbsp. chopped Italian parsley
1 tsp. fresh oregano, chopped
pinch crushed rosemary leaves
2 tbs. brandy
1/3 cup dry white wine
1 cup evaporated skim milk
2 dashes Worcestershire sauce
1 Tbsp. low calorie margarine softened
white pepper to taste

1   On each of four skewers, put three each of the scallops, shrimp, and Canadian bacon. Fold the Canadian bacon in quarters, or fold them in half over a scallop or a shrimp. This is best cooked over an open fire on a rotisserie, but it can also be cooked under the broiler.

2   To make the sauce, spray skillet with olive oil. Saute the onions and garlic until light brown around the edges. Add the crushed red pepper, basil, parsley, oregano and rosemary. Carefully add the brandy and touch a flame to it. Add the wine, bring to a boil, and reduce by half.

3   Add the evaporated skim milk and Worcestershire and reduce by about one-fourth. Whisk in the margarine. Add white pepper to taste. Strain the sauce and serve 2 Tbsp. on each of four platters.

4   Place the skewers on the plate and pull them out of the seafood.
Serves four.

NUTRITIONAL INFORMATION PER SERVING
180 Calories
5 gm. fat
49 mg Cholesterol
750 mg. sodium

Pesce Rosso Arlecchino

Harlequin Redfish

4 Redfish fillets, 3 oz. each
Fish marinade
1/2 onion, sliced
1 cup mixed red, green, and yellow bell pepper, thinly sliced
1 tsp. minced garlic
Pinch crushed red pepper
1/2 cup dry white wine
1 cup fish stock
1 Tbsp. lemon juice
Leaves from 2 sprigs of fresh oregano
1/2 tsp. Worcestershire
1 ripe tomato, peeled and seeded, coarsely chopped

Preheat oven to 400 degrees.

1 Wash the fish under cold water and pat dry. Marinate the fish for a minute or two on each side in the marinade. Sprinkle the fillets lightly with pepper, and flour.

2 Spray skillet with olive oil. Saute the fish for about one minute, then turn. Put the skillet into a preheated 400-degree oven and bake for about five minutes. Do not allow the fish to dry out or crack. Remove the fish to serving plates and keep it warm.

3 Spray same skillet with olive oil. Saute onions, bell peppers, garlic and crushed red pepper until onions turn translucent.

4 Add wine and bring to a boil. Add fish stock, lemon juice, oregano, Worcestershire, and tomato. Return to a boil and cook until peppers have just lost their crispness, but are still al dente. Drape peppers and onions across fish and pour liquid part of sauce around fish. Garnish with fresh oregano.

Serves four.

NUTRITIONAL INFORMATION PER SERVING
270 Calories
7 gm. fat
45 mg. cholesterol
349 mg. sodium

Tonno Giulia

Tuna With Fennel

1/2 head fresh fennel, sliced
1 Tbs. fennel seeds, dry
2 tuna steaks (about 4 oz. each)
1/2 Tbs. extra virgin olive oil
1/4 cup leeks, chopped
1/4 cup carrots, chopped
1/4 cup white wine
1/4 cup fish stock
4 drops Tabasco
1/8 tsp. Worcestershire
Juice of one fresh lemon
Salt and pepper as needed
2 sprigs Italian parsley, chopped

1   Soak dry fennel seeds in water for one hour.
2   Rub fennel seeds on top of each tuna steak. Saute the tuna in olive oil in a hot skillet, cooking two minutes each side until done.
3   Add all other ingredients and bring to a boil. Lower heat and simmer for five minutes, until very little liquid is left. Serve fish with sauce and chopped parsley.
Serves two.

NUTRITION INFORMATION PER SERVING
237 calories
5 gm. fat
Less than 1 gm. saturated fat
188 mg. sodium

Salmone Lesso

Poached Salmon

1/4 cup white wine
Juice of 1/2 lemon
2 sprigs Italian parsley, chopped
2 leaves celery, chopped
1/4 medium onion, chopped
4 sprigs dill
1/4 tsp. salt
1 Tbs. white vinegar
4 oz. fresh salmon fillet

Sauce:
1 tsp. margarine
1 tsp. chopped onion
1/4 tsp. chopped garlic
4 sprigs fresh dill (1/2 tsp. dry dill)
1 Tbs. dry vermouth
1 Tbs. white wine
1/4 cup fish stock
1/4 cup skimmed evaporated milk
1/8 tsp. salt
1/8 tsp. Tabasco
1/8 tsp. Worcestershire

1 In a sauce pan under high heat, combine one quart water with white wine, lemon juice, parsley, celery, onion, dill, salt and vinegar. Bring to a light boil and hold for one hour.

2 Lower heat, add salmon and continue to simmer for six minutes.

3 In a separate skillet under medium heat, brown onion and garlic in margarine. Add fresh dill, vermouth, wine and stock. Reduce for 10 minutes.

4 Add skimmed evaporated milk and bring to a boil then reduce again.

5 Add the salt, Tabasco and Worcestershire.

6 Serve 1/2 cup of the sauce over the salmon fillet with your favorite accompaniments.

Serves one.

NUTRITION INFORMATION PER SERVING
234 calories
8 gm. fat
2 gm. saturated fat
392 mg. sodium

Rombo Oreganata

Flounder With Fresh Herb Sauce

1/4 cup white wine
Juice of 1/2 lemon
2 sprigs Italian parsley, chopped
2 leaves celery, chopped
1/4 medium onion, chopped
4 sprigs dill
1/4 tsp. salt
1 Tbs. white vinegar
4 oz. fresh flounder fillet

Sauce:

1/2 tsp. margarine
1/2 Tbs. chopped onion
1 tsp. chopped garlic
1 Tbs. capers, chopped
1 Tbs. dry vermouth
1 Tbs. white wine
1/4 cup fish stock
1 Tbs. fresh chopped oregano
1 Tbs. fresh Italian parsley
2 medium mushrooms, sliced
1/4 tsp. salt

1 In a saucepan under high heat, combine one quart water with white wine, lemon juice, parsley, celery, onion, dill, salt and vinegar. Bring to a light boil and hold for about 15 minutes.

2 Lower heat, add flounder and simmer for six minutes. Remove carefully with a turner. Drain and keep warm.

3 In a separate skillet over medium heat, saute the onion and garlic in margarine. Add the capers, vermouth, wine, stock, oregano, parsley, mushrooms and salt. Bring to a boil and cook until very little liquid remains.

4 Serve sauce over flounder with half lemon.
Serves one.

NUTRITION INFORMATION PER SERVING
206 calories
3 gm. fat
0 gm. saturated fat
335 mg. sodium

"Amberjack" Saltato Con Aglio
Sauteed Amberjack With Garlic

Fish marinade:
2 Tbs. extra-virgin olive oil
1 Tbs. dry white wine
1/2 tsp. lemon juice
Dash Worcestershire sauce
2 drops Tabasco

2 (4 oz.) fresh amberjack fillets
1 tsp. vegetable oil
Flour

Sauce:
1 tsp. extra virgin olive oil
2 garlic cloves, smashed with back of knife
1/4 cup red wine
1/4 cup fish stock
1/4 tsp. crushed red pepper
1/8 tsp. salt
1 tsp. fresh Italian parsley, chopped

1   Dip amberjack fillets in the fish marinade for about 30 seconds on each side. Let excess marinade drip off. Lightly dust fish with flour.

2   In a skillet under medium heat, saute one side of the amberjack fillets in vegetable oil for 2-3 minutes. Then place in a preheated oven at 450 degrees for eight minutes.

3   In the same skillet, saute garlic in olive oil until golden brown. Add remaining ingredients except for the parsley and bring to a boil. Remove from heat and add the parsley when liquids are reduced by half. Serve sauce over the amberjack with garlic clove on top.

Serves two.

NUTRITION INFORMATION PER SERVING
191 calories
7 gm. fat
0 gm. saturated fat
150 mg. sodium

Vongole In Umido

Steamed Clams

24 fresh clams, in shells
1 Tbs. olive oil
1/4 cup chopped onion
2 tsp. chopped fresh garlic
1/2 tsp. crushed red pepper
1/2 cup dry white wine
1 cup fish stock
2 tsp. chopped Italian parsley
1/4 tsp. white pepper
4 cups linguiine, cooked al dente

1 Check the clams to make sure all of them are tightly closed. If you find one that's slightly agape, tap it lightly with a spoon; if it doesn't close, it's dead or worse. Throw it away.

2 Scrub clams well and rinse them with cold water.

3 In a large skillet, heat olive oil over medium heat and saute onion and garlic until onions are blond. Add crushed red pepper, wine, stock, parsley, and pepper. Bring to a boil.

4 Add clams in shell. Cover skillet and let clams steam for 10 minutes. Remove cover and agitate skillet to slosh sauce inside the clam shells, which will have opened.

5 Taste sauce and adjust seasonings. You probably will not need to add salt, since the clams are usually rather salty already.

Makes eight appetizers or four entrees. If serving as an entree, accompany with cooked linguine tossed with extra sauce and garnished with chopped parsley.

NUTRITION INFORMATION PER SERVING
(Entree portion with linguine)
200 calories
5 gm. fat
Less than 1 gm. saturated fat
66 mg. sodium

Cozze O Vongole Alla Marinara

Mussels or Clams Marinara

24 fresh mussels or clams, in the shell, prepared "in umido" (see previous recipe)
2 tsp. chopped Italian parsley
1 Tbs. fresh oregano leaves
2 cups canned Italian plum tomatoes, chopped
1 cup juice from tomatoes
1 Tbs. chopped fresh basil
Salt and pepper, as needed
4 cups linguine, cooked al dente

1   After preparing steamed clams or mussels according to the Vongole in Umido recipe, remove them from the skillet and add all the other ingredients in this recipe.

2   Bring the skillet to a boil, then lower heat and simmer for 15-20 minutes, until reduced by about a third.

3   Return mussels or clams to the skillet, and toss with the marinara sauce.

Makes eight appetizers or four entrees. If serving as an entree, accompany with cooked linguine tossed with extra sauce and garnished with chopped parsley.

NUTRITION INFORMATION PER SERVING
(Entree portion with linguine)
266 calories
2 gm. fat
0 gm. saturated fat
376 mg. sodium

Gamberi Caprese

Shrimp Capri Style

1 Tbs. extra virgin olive oil
1 Tbs. chopped onion
1/2 tsp. chopped garlic
Pinch crushed red pepper
6 medium shrimp, peeled and deveined
1/2 Tbs. brandy
1/4 cup dry white wine
1/2 cup fish stock
1/2 tsp. chopped Italian parsley
1/2 tsp. chopped fresh basil leaves
1/2 tsp. chopped fresh oregano
1/2 tsp. fresh rosemary leaves
1 Tbs. lemon juice
3 drops Tabasco
1 tsp. Worcestershire sauce
1/4 tsp. salt
Pinch white pepper
1 cup cooked angel hair pasta

1   Heat oil in a saute pan until very hot. Saute onion, garlic, and crushed red pepper until lightly browned.

2   Add shrimp and saute until pink.

3   Add brandy and carefully flame it. When flames die down, remove shrimp and keep warm. Add white wine and fish stock. Bring to a boil, then add all the other ingredients.

4   Return the shrimp to the pan and simmer in the sauce for about 30 seconds on each side. Take the shrimp out of the pan and arrange on a plate, then pour the sauce over them. This can be served with angel hair pasta.

Serves two.

NUTRITION INFORMATION PER SERVING
244 calories
8 gm. fat
1 gm. saturated fat
350 mg. sodium

Gamberi Saltati Bayou Lafourche

Shrimp Saute Bayou Lafourche

6 shrimp, 21-25 count, peeled and deveined but with tails still on
1 tsp. extra virgin olive oil
1 tsp. chopped shallots
1 tsp. chopped garlic
1/4 tsp. crushed red pepper
1 Tbs. brandy
1/4 cup dry white wine
1/4 tsp. Worcestershire
Juice of 1/2 lemon
1/2 tsp. fresh rosemary leaves
1/4 tsp. salt
Pinch white pepper
Pinch cayenne

1 Heat the olive oil in a saute pan under medium heat. Saute the shallots, garlic, and crushed red pepper until shallots are transparent.

2 Add the shrimp, and cook, turning once, until shrimp are pink.

3 Add the brandy and flame it. Remove the shrimp and keep warm.

4 Add wine, Worcestershire, lemon juice, rosemary, salt, pepper, and cayenne. Lower the heat and simmer for 10 minutes, until reduced by a third.

5 Return shrimp to the pan and cook for three or four minutes more, coating well with sauce.

Serves two appetizers or one entree. If serving as an entree, accompany with your favorite pasta side dish.

NUTRITION INFORMATION PER SERVING
(Appetizer portion)
105 calories
3 gm. fat
0 gm. saturated fat
221 mg. sodium

Scampi Fra Diavolo

Jumbo Shrimp "Brother Devil"

1 Tbs. extra virgin olive oil
24 fresh shrimp, 10-15 count to the pound, peeled and deveined
2 Tbs. chopped onion
1 Tbs. chopped garlic
1 1/2 tsp. crushed red pepper
2 Tbs. brandy
1/2 cup dry white wine
1/4 cup chopped Italian plum tomatoes, with juice
1 Tbs. chopped fresh oregano
8 leaves chopped fresh basil
1/4 tsp. white pepper

1   In a skillet, heat the olive oil over medium heat. Saute the onions, garlic, and crushed red pepper until lightly browned. Put the shrimp in the pan and saute for about a minute, making sure liquid ingredients in the pan cover them.

2   Add brandy and carefully flame it. When flames die out, add white wine and bring to a boil. When shrimp are pink and firm, remove from skillet and keep warm.

3   Add tomato to skillet and bring to a boil. Lower heat, add oregano and basil, and simmer for about five minutes, or until sauce has thickened to about the consistency of vegetable soup. Add salt and pepper to taste.

4   Return the shrimp to the pan and simmer another five minutes Serve six shrimp per person with plenty of sauce.

Serves four.

NUTRITION INFORMATION PER SERVING
265 calories
14 gm. fat
2 gm. saturated fat
220 mg. sodium

Gamberi Michelle

Shrimp With Herbed Yogurt Sauce

1/2 Tbs. olive oil
1 tsp. chopped onion
1/2 tsp. chopped garlic
1 lb. (21-25 count) fresh shrimp, tails on, heads off
1 Tbs. brandy
1 Tbs. sherry
4 drops Tabasco
1/2 Tbs. green onion, chopped
1/2 tsp. fresh oregano, chopped
1/2 tsp. fresh basil, chopped
4 oz. low-fat yogurt
Salt and pepper to taste
1/2 cup cooked rice

1 Heat the olive oil in a skillet until it shimmers. Add the onions and garlic and saute until soft.

2 Add the shrimp and saute until they turn pink and firm—about three minutes.

3 Add the brandy and carefully touch a flame to it. When flames subside, add the sherry and simmer for additional five minutes. Add green onions, oregano, and basil and remove from heat.

4 While the step above is happening, in a separate saucepan warm the yogurt and stir until it has a smooth consistency. Let cool.

5 Add the yogurt to the shrimp. Agitate the pan to combine all the ingredients. Serve over rice.

Serves one.

NUTRITION INFORMATION PER SERVING
370 calories
9 gm. fat
2 gm. saturated fat
564 mg. sodium

Salmone Dannon

Salmon With Yogurt Sauce

4 fresh salmon fillets, about 4 oz. each

Sauce:
1/2 tsp. fresh dill, chopped
1 tsp. Dijon mustard
1 cup low-fat yogurt
1/2 tsp. honey
1/8 tsp. Tabasco

1   In a saucepan over medium high heat, heat 1 quart water until boiling. Reduce heat.

2   Add salmon fillets and simmer for 6-8 minutes. Remove the fish and keep warm.

3   While the salmon is simmering, prepare the sauce. In a saucepan, heat the yogurt under low heat to a smooth consistency. Remove from the heat and let cool. Add mustard, dill, and honey.

4   Place salmon fillet on a leaf of fresh spinach or Boston bibb lettuce. Pour approximately two ounces of sauce on top of the salmon and serve with your favorite vegetable.

Serves four.

NUTRITION INFORMATION PER SERVING
270 calories
6 gm. fat
2 gm. saturated fat
209 mg. sodium

Cacciucco Alla Livornese (Cioppino)

Seafood Stew with Saffron

1 Tbs. extra virgin olive oil
1 Tbs. chopped onion
1 tsp. chopped garlic
4 clams in shells, well washed
4 mussels in shells, well washed and debearded
1/4 tsp. crushed red pepper
1/2 cup dry white wine
1/2 cup fish stock
2 cans Italian plum tomatoes with juice
4 medium shrimp
4 medium large oysters
4 scallops
4 calamari, cleaned and sliced
1/4 tsp. salt
Pinch white pepper
1 tsp. fresh basil leaves, chopped
1 tsp. fresh oregano, chopped
1 tsp. chopped Italian parsley
3 drops Tabasco
1/4 tsp. Worcestershire
2 oz. trout fillet, sliced
2 portions cooked linguine

1 Heat olive oil in a saucepan until very hot. Saute onions and garlic until lightly browned. Add the clams, mussels, crushed red pepper and white wine. Cover and steam the shellfish until they open. (The mussels will open first).

2 Remove from pan and put them into a quart of warm water with one tsp. salt. Wash the sand out and remove any beards off the mussels.

3 While the shellfish are soaking, add the fish stock and tomatoes to the pan and bring to a boil. Add the shrimp, oysters, scallops, and calamari and cook over medium-low heat.

4 When the pan returns to boil, add the salt, pepper, basil, oregano, parsley, Tabasco and Worcestershire. Cook another three minutes then add the trout, clams and mussels. Cook for another three minutes, until the trout begins to flake.

5 Place the clams and mussels around the edge of a large platter. Place the linguine in the center of the plate, and pour the rest of the contents of the pan onto the plate.

Serves two.

NUTRITION INFORMATION PER SERVING
363 calories
9 gm. fat
1 gm. saturated fat
464 mg. sodium

Cappe Sante Al Dragoncello

Scallops with Tarragon Sauce

1 tsp. extra virgin olive oil
1 Tbs. chopped onions
1 tsp. chopped garlic
Pinch crushed red pepper
12 medium-large scallops (12 oz. total)
1/4 cup dry vermouth
1/4 cup dry white wine
1/4 cup fish stock
1/2 Tbs. fresh tarragon leaves
Dash Tabasco
1/4 tsp. Worcestershire
1/4 tsp. salt
Pinch white pepper
1 Tbs. skimmed evaporated milk

1 Heat olive oil in a saute pan over medium heat. Saute onions, garlic, and crushed red pepper until lightly browned.

2 Add scallops and saute for one minute. Remove the scallops and keep them warm. Add the vermouth, white wine, and fish stock. Bring to a boil and reduce the liquid by a third.

3 Strain the sauce through a sieve into another skillet over medium heat. Return the scallops and add the tarragon, Tabasco, Worcestershire, salt and pepper.

4 When bubbles reappear in the sauce, add the skimmed evaporated milk. Cook for another minute or so. Don't overcook; the scallops should still bulge a bit when completely cooked.

5 Remove the scallops again and slice them into butterflies. Arrange them on serving plates. Continue to reduce the sauce for another minute, then remove from heat. Spoon the sauce over the scallops.

Makes four appetizers or two entrees. If serving as an entree, serve with saffron rice.

NUTRITION INFORMATION PER SERVING
(Appetizer portion)
59 calories
1 gm. fat
0 gm. saturated fat
200 mg. sodium

Meats

Petto Di Tachino Farcito

Turkey Breast Belvedere

4 oz. turkey breast, pounded thin
5 leaves fresh spinach
5 strips bell pepper
2 whole mushrooms, sliced
4 green beans
1/2 tsp. oregano
1/2 tsp. fresh basil
1 tsp. vegetable oil
1/4 cup tomato basil sauce (see page 00)

1 Assemble the spinach, bell pepper, mushrooms, and green beans on top of the turkey breast. Sprinkle with the fresh herbs. Roll the turkey breast using butcher's string. Wrap the string around the breast before cooking.
2 Add a pinch of salt and pepper, then dust the turkey roll with flour.
3 Place the vegetable oil in a skillet and brown the turkey roll on all sides.
4 Bake at 400 degrees for approximately 10 minutes.
5 Remove string, cut turkey roll into six slices and serve on top of 1/4 cup of tomato basil sauce.
Serves one.

NUTRITIONAL INFORMATION PER SERVING
216 Calories
8 gm. fat
2 gm. of saturated fat
70 mg. sodium

Paillards

The word "paillard" is French, but the style is much seen and admired in Italian cookery. It consists of grilling or broiling a thin, broad piece of meat very quickly with high heat. The result is served with the lightest of sauces, such as the herb sauce I suggest here.

The meat you use can be turkey breast, beef round, white veal leg, or chicken breast. The procedure, once you have pounded the meat out to a thin cutlet, is the same.

4 oz. unsliced turkey breast, beef round, veal leg, or chicken breast
1 tsp. olive oil
1 tsp. extra virgin olive oil
1/2 tsp. chopped Italian parsley
Juice of 1/2 lemon, strained

1   Using wax paper to wrap the meat, pound out the meat until it is thin but not falling apart.

2   Brush olive oil on both sides of the meat.

3   Place the meat on a very hot grill or under a preheated broiler and cook for two minutes (at most!) on the first side and one minute on the second side.

4   Combine the extra virgin olive oil and chopped Italian parsley. Pour this mixture over the cooked meat and add the lemon juice over the top.

5   Serve with your favorite pasta and vegetables.
Serves one.

NUTRITION INFORMATION PER SERVING
Turkey:
236 calories
12 gm. fat
2 gm. saturated fat
63 mg. sodium

Chicken breast:
244 calories
12 gm. fat
2 gm. saturated fat
84 mg. sodium

Veal:
182 calories
14 gm. fat
3 gm. saturated fat
63 mg. sodium

Beef round:
262 calories
14 gm. fat
5 gm. saturated fat
65 mg. sodium

Risotto con Pollo

Chicken Risotto

1 chicken breast, boneless and skinless, cubed (3 oz.)
1 tsp. chopped onions
1/4 tsp. chopped garlic
2 sprigs Italian parsley, chopped
1 tsp. fresh rosemary leaves, chopped
1 pinch crushed red pepper
1/8 cup dry white wine
1/2 cup chicken stock
1/2 cup Basic Risotto
1 Tbsp. part-skim Parmesan cheese
Pinch white pepper

Preheat oven to 450 degrees.

1 Spray skillet with olive oil. Saute the chicken breast until it turns white. Add the onions, garlic, parsley, rosemary, and crushed red pepper, and saute until onions are blond.

2 Add white wine and bring to a boil. Add chicken stock and return to a boil. Add the Risotto and heat through. Remove from the heat.

3 Stir in the part-skim Parmesan cheese, and pepper.
Serves one entree.

NUTRITIONAL INFORMATION PER SERVING
330 Calories
5 gm. fat
77 mg. cholesterol
449 mg. sodium

Pollo Valdostana

Chicken Valdostana

10 large leaves fresh spinach
1 skinless chicken breasts, 3 oz. each
1 ounce Prosciutto
1 ounce part-skim mozzarella cheese
2 fresh basil leaves
1/4 cup flour
pinch white pepper
2 egg whites
1/8 cup bread crumbs

Sauce:
1 tsp. chopped onion
1/2 tsp. chopped garlic
1/4 tsp. fresh rosemary leaves
pinch white pepper
2 Tbsp. dry white wine
1/4 cup chicken stock
1/4 tsp. chopped Italian parsley
1 Tbsp. low-calorie margarine

Preheat oven to 400 degrees.

1 Bring a pot of water to a boil and briefly poach the spinach leaves - no more than 30 seconds - and plunge them into cold water.

2 Pound skinless chicken breasts to uniform thickness. Cover the surface of the chicken with spinach leaves. Top that with mozzarella, prosciutto, and basil. Fold the chicken breast over in thirds.

3 Dust these chicken "packages" with the flour and pepper. Pass them through the egg whites, then coat lightly with bread crumbs.

4 Spray skillet with olive oil and saute chicken on one side for about a minute, until lightly brown. Turn the chicken and put the entire skillet into the oven for 10 minutes.

5 Meanwhile, prepare the sauce. Spray skillet with olive oil. Over medium heat saute onions and garlic until blond. Add the rosemary, pepper, wine and chicken stock, and bring to a boil. Reduce by half, then take the pan off the stove. Whisk the margarine into the sauce.

6 Spoon the sauce over the chicken and top with parsley
Serves two.

NUTRITIONAL INFORMATION PER SERVING
350 Calories
10 gm. fat
88.5 mg. cholesterol
492 mg. sodium

Pollo al Forno Della Nonna

Grandmothers Baked Chicken

4 (4 oz.) chicken breasts
1/2 large onion
1/2 large carrot
1 rib celery
2 sprigs fresh rosemary
white pepper
1/2 tsp. chopped fresh garlic
1/4 dry white wine
2 cups chicken stock
2 medium-large mushrooms

Preheat oven to 450 degrees.

1   Skin and debone the chicken breasts and pound them out to uniform thickness.
2   Spray skillet with olive oil. Cook breasts one to two minutes until lightly browned on both sides. Put skillet with chicken breasts into the oven for 15 minutes. Put to the side.
3   Chop onion, carrot and celery into large chunks (about an inch long.) Reserve two or three pieces of each; chop these into slivers.
4   Spray skillet with olive oil. Put vegetables in skillet, along with garlic, white wine, chicken stock, rosemary and a pinch of white pepper.
5   Cook for about two minutes, then remove vegetables and puree in food processor or blender. Meanwhile, reduce liquid in skillet to about half. Return puree to skillet and stir in. Then add slivered fresh vegetables reserved earlier and quartered mushrooms; cook about two minutes, leaving vegetables crisp. Your sauce is now complete and may be distributed evenly over the chicken breasts.
   Serves four.

NUTRITIONAL INFORMATION PER SERVING
206 Calories.
4 gm. fat
85 mg. cholesterol
378 mg. sodium

Osso Buco Milanese
Braised Veal Shanks in Brown Sauce

8 slices veal round, cut 1-1/2 inches thick (3 oz. each)
Sprinkles of pepper and flour
1 lb. veal bones, cut one inch long
2 ribs celery, cubed
1 medium onion, cubed
1 cup chopped carrots
3 garlic cloves, lightly crushed
1/2 cup chopped leek
2 Tbsp. tomato paste
1-1/2 cups dry red wine
1/3 cup flour
4 leaves fresh sage
1 tsp. dry marjoram
2 sprigs Italian parsley
1/2 tsp. dried thyme
2 bay leaves
2 short sprigs fresh rosemary
1/2 tsp. salt
1/4 tsp. white pepper

Brunoise:
Chop these vegetables coarsely:
1/2 carrot
1/4 onion
1 rib celery
1/4 leek (white part only)

Preheat the oven to 450 degrees.

1   Sprinkle pepper and flour over the veal shanks. Spray skillet with olive oil. Put veal in and brown on both sides. Remove from saucepan and drain shanks.

2   In the same saucepan, brown the veal bones over high flame. May spray skillet with olive oil as needed. After meat on bones is a medium brown, add celery, onion, carrots, leeks and garlic cloves. When edges of onion start to brown, add tomato paste and red wine and continue to cook over high heat, stirring frequently.

3   When liquid reduces by a little more than half (you will now have an appealing, red-brown sauce in the pan), sprinkle in flour and stir well. When flour is completely blended, add one gallon of water and stir. Add sage, marjoram, parsley, thyme, bay and rosemary.

4   When pot returns to boil, put veal in and put the entire saucepan into a preheated 450-degree oven.

5   After an hour and 15 minutes, check the veal for doneness. It is completely cooked when a kitchen fork can be inserted deep into the meat and pulled back out without resistance. When it reaches that point, remove veal from sauce and reserve.

6 Put saucepan full of stock back on a hot fire and continue to reduce. After 30 minutes, skim top of pot to remove foam and fat. Strain stock through cheesecloth.

7 Return stock to a medium simmer and return veal shanks into it. Add salt and pepper.

8 Using a sieve to hold them, boil the brunoise vegetables in about a quart of water for about a minute. Add the brunoise to the stock and cook another three or four minutes, until sauce is the desired thickness. It is the style in many restaurants around New Orleans to make the sauce of osso buco so thick that you can eat it with a fork. But this is not the way it is done in Italy, where the sauce is very light, yet no less flavorful. In any case, the osso buco should be served with the bone upright and lots of the sauce. Angel hair pasta is a perfect accompaniment, moistened with the sauce.

Serves eight.

NUTRITIONAL INFORMATION PER SERVING
324 Calories
10 gm. fat
88 mg. cholesterol
226 mg. sodium

Bistecca Pizzaiola
Steak with Spicy Tomato Sauce

4 strip sirloin steaks, 3 oz. each
4 cloves garlic, sliced very thin (not chopped)
1 Tbsp. chopped onion
1/2 cup red wine
1/2 tsp. crushed red pepper
8 canned Italian plum tomatoes, plus 1 cup of juice (no added salt)
2 sprigs oregano leaves, chopped
1/2 tsp. salt
pinch white pepper

1 Trim excess fat from sirloin. Dust with salt and pepper, and pound with your fist to spread it out a little.

2 Spray skillet with olive oil and put the steak in to brown for about two minutes on each side. Add garlic and onions and saute with steak about a minute more. Remove steak, which will now be medium rare.

3 Add red wine, crushed red pepper, tomatoes, and tomato juice, and bring to a boil. Add parsley and oregano. Reduce heat to medium low, and simmer for five minutes.

4 Serve about four ounces of sauce over each steak.
Serves four.

NUTRITIONAL INFORMATION PER SERVING
218 Calories
8 gm. fat
76 mg Cholesterol
527 mg. sodium

Filetto di Manzo Andrea

Filet Mignon with Mushrooms

4 filet mignons, 3 oz. each
1 tbs. chopped onion
1/2 Tbsp. chopped garlic
1/2 cup red and green bell pepper, chopped
8 medium mushrooms, sliced
1/2 tsp. cracked black pepper
1/3 cup brandy
1 cup dry white wine
1 cup au jus
1 cup evaporated skim milk
1/4 tsp. salt
pinch white pepper

1   Slice the filets across into two medallions, but leave them hinged.

2   Spray skillet with olive oil. Put steaks in two at a time and cook for two minutes on each side for medium rare. Remove steaks and keep warm.

3   In the same skillet, saute all vegetables until tender, adding them to the pan in the order given above. Add brandy and carefully ignite it. Let the flame burn out, then add wine and bring to a boil for about two minutes.

4   Reduce sauce by half. Add au jus, evaporated skim milk, salt and pepper. Return to a boil and reduce by about a third.

5   Return filets (two at a time) to sauce and cook till heated through - about 15 seconds. Remove to plates with about three ounces of sauce on each.

Serves four.

NUTRITIONAL INFORMATION PER SERVING
279 Calories
8 gm. fat
78 mg. cholesterol
423 mg. sodium

Polo alla Cacciatore

Hunter's Chicken

1 cup flour
1/2 tsp. salt
1/4 tsp. white pepper
24 oz. chicken pieces
1/2 cup chopped onion
1 tsp. chopped garlic
2 sprigs fresh rosemary (leaves only)
1/2 tsp. crushed red pepper
1 cup dry white wine
6 cups canned Italian plum tomatoes (no added salt)
2 cups juice from canned tomatoes (no added salt)
2 bay leaves
16 medium fresh mushrooms
1 tsp. chopped Italian parsley

Preheat oven to 450 degrees.

1   In a bowl, mix flour, salt and pepper and coat chicken with it.
2   Spray skillet with olive oil and in it cook chicken pieces for three to five minutes, until lightly browned. Remove chicken and keep warm.
3   Spray skillet with olive oil. Add the onion, garlic, rosemary, and crushed red pepper. Saute until onions turn blond. Add wine and bring to a light boil.
4   With clean hands, squeeze tomatoes through fingers into the saucepan with the extra juice. Bring sauce back to a boil and add chicken pieces. Add white pepper to taste and bay leaves. Return to a boil, then put entire saucepan into a preheated 450-degree oven. Cook for about 45 minutes, until chicken is tender.
5   Take saucepan from oven, and remove chicken. Stir mushrooms and parsley into sauce and cook over medium heat until both are incorporated into sauce - about two minutes. Serve immediately.
    Serves eight.

NUTRITIONAL INFORMATION PER SERVING
290 Calories
6 gm. fat
73 mg. cholesterol
231 mg. sodium

Arista di Maiale ai Funghi
Port Tenderloin with Chanterelle Sauce

1 pork tenderloin, about 6 oz.
1/4 cup dry white wine

Sauce:
2 cups fresh chanterelle mushrooms
1 Tbsp. chopped onions
1 tsp. chopped garlic
1 cup pork sauce
1/2 tsp. salt
pinch white pepper
1/2 tsp. chopped fresh sage

Preheat oven to 450 degrees.

1   Spray skillet with olive oil. Saute the pork tenderloin, turning every minute or so, until browned on the outside. Add the wine and 1/2 cup water and bring to a boil. Then put the skillet into a preheated 450 degree oven.

2   Meanwhile, make the sauce. Spray skillet with olive oil. Saute the onions and garlic until light brown around the edges. Add the chanterelles and saute until the mushrooms become tender on the outside - which happens in less than a minute over high heat.

3   Add the pork stock* to the sauce skillet and toss with the mushrooms to coat. Bring to a boil, then add the sage.

4   The pork tenderloin is done when a meat thermometer pushed into the center registers 140 degrees. Slice the pork tenderloin diagonally into slices about 1/4 inch thick.

5   Serve pork, napped with about 1/4 cup of the sauce.
    Serves two.

*See pork sauce recipe.

NUTRITIONAL INFORMATION PER SERVING
257 Calories
7.5 gm. fat
80 mg Cholesterol
499 mg. sodium

Pollo con Salsa Bianca
Chicken with White Sauce

12 oz. skinless chicken pieces
1 medium onion, cut up
1 stalk celery, cut up
3 bay leaves
1 Tbsp. low calorie margarine
3 Tbsp. all-purpose flour
1/2 tsp. salt
1/8 cup evaporated skim milk
1/2 leek, white part only, chopped
1/8 cup red bell pepper, sliced

1 Put the skinless chicken pieces in a sauce pan with 2 quarts cold water. Add the onion, celery, and bay leaves. Bring to a boil, then boil chicken 35 minutes. Remove from water and cool.

2 Bring stock to a boil and reduce water to one-quarter its original volume. Strain the stock.

3 In a skillet, make a blond roux with the low calorie margarine and flour. Add the stock to the roux and briskly whisk. Reduce by about one-third.

4 Add the chicken to the sauce and simmer until it's heated through.

5 Strain off 1-1/2 cups of the reduced chicken sauce. Add salt. Heat it in a skillet till bubbling, then add the evaporated skim milk and the leek. Saute until the leek is tender. Nap over the chicken. Garnish with strips of red bell pepper.

Serves four.

NUTRITIONAL INFORMATION PER SERVING
206 Calories
5 gm. fat
73 mg Cholesterol
390 mg. sodium

Axis Venison Casserole

20 0z. venison meat-cut in cubes
4 oz. diced celery
2 oz. fresh tomatoes diced
16 oz. water or beef stock
1 tbls. red currant jelly
salt & pepper to taste
4 oz. diced carrots
5 oz. chopped onions
3 cloves of garlic chopped
1 qt. red wine
1 tbls. low fat sour cream

Marinate venison 24 hours in the following:
1 qt. red wine
1 doz. black peppercorn
3 bay leaves
6 juniper berries

Remove meat from marinade, reserving the liquid.

1 In a deep saute pan heat 1 tbls. olive oil on low to medium. Add
venison and saute till nicely browned. Remove meat from pan. In same pan
saute carrots, celery, onions & garlic till transparent. Add reserved marinade
liquid, plus 16 oz. water or beef stock. Bring to a boil.
2 Add venison, tomatoes, and bay leaves from marinade. Bring back to a
boil. Lower heat to medium and simmer for 1 hour and 25 minutes or bake at
450 degrees.
3 If more liquid is needed add beef stock or water to desired consistence.
When fully cooked remove from heat, add sour cream and currant jelly and
stir. To serve place 3 oz. white rice on plate, make hole in the middle of rice
and add venison mixture.

Serves 4

P.S. I like to use the shoulder cut of venison.

NUTRITIONAL INFORMATION PER SERVING
430 Calories
5 gm. fat
1 gm. of saturated fat
350 mg. sodium

Venison Sausage

2 lbs. lean pork tenders
1 1/2 oz. black peppercorns
1/2 oz. thyme
4 oz. chopped onion
1/2 oz. olive oil
2 oz. brandy
1/2 oz. sage
12 juniper berries
1/2 oz. margarine
4 lbs. venison meat
1/2 oz. marjoram
4 oz. chopped italian parsley
1 oz. chopped garlic
1 oz. madeira wine
1/4 tsp. nutmeg
1 bay leave
1/2 tsp. salt

Marinade

12 qts. red wine
6 juniper berries
1 doz. peppercorns
9 bay leaves

1 Marinate venison in marinade mixture 24 hours
2 Remove from marinade & proceed
3 Saute onions & garlic in the 2 oz. of olive oil & low fat butter till transparent. Add brandy, madeira wine, and 4 oz. of liquid strained from marinade. Bring to a boil, remove from the heat & let stand till cool. Add venison & pork. Stir well. Add all other herbs and spices. Mix again.
4 Place all ingredients in meat grinder using fine grind. Add funnel attachment to grinder. Place casing over the funnel and start the grinder on low speed. Fill casings using one hand to form shape and using the other hand to feed the grinder using stomper to advance the meat through grinder.
5 Saute in skillet in small amount of olive oil over low heat, browning on all sides for 2 minutes. Place skillet in oven at 400 degrees for 10 minutes or until firm.

Makes 5 pounds of sausage (Approximately 20 servings).

NUTRITIONAL INFORMATION PER SERVING
267 Calories
10 gm. fat
3 gm. of saturated fat
350 mg. sodium

Medallions of Venison, Christmas Style

I originally developed this sauce for my own family's Christmas Dinner and I have served it every Christmas since. (I would be in trouble if I decided to skip it one year.) The sauce evolved over the years as I experimented with it. The sour cream, for example, took the place of whipping cream one year because I had just cooked a lot of german food at the hotel of which I was working. I thought the sour cream made a great improvement in the sauce.

Not only is this a fantastic complement to any cut of venison, it also goes very well with turkey, duck, or a veal chop. This recipe makes quite a bit of this sauce, which you can refrigerate or freeze for a future use. Just leave out the sour cream from the portion you will be saving, and add it when you're ready to serve the sauce again.

As for the venison itself, I am finding it more widely available since they started raising axis deer commercially in Texas. In southeast Louisiana, a lot of people hunt deer and wind up with more of it than they know what to do with. Here's what.

3 lbs. venison bones, cut up
5 oz. extra virgin olive oil
2 ribs of celery
2 cloves garlic, sliced
1 tbs. juniper berries (broken)
1/2 cup of flour
1/2 tsp marjoram
1 tsp. salt
1/2 cup currant jelly

1/2 cup peanut oil
1 carrot
1 medium onion, cut up
1/3 cup tomato paste
3 cups dry red wine
1/2 tsp. thyme
2 bay leaves
1/4 tsp. white pepper
1/2 cup low fat sour cream

1 Put the bones, peanut & olive oil into a large stockpot. Brown over high heat for 20 minutes. Add the carrot, celery, onion, & garlic. Cook for about 20 minutes, until bones are thoroughly and darkly browned.

2 Add tomato paste, juniper berries, and red wine. Allow liquids to reduce by half.

3 Sprinkle flour into pot. Stir contents to brown flour lightly. Add a gallon of water and thoroughly stir contents of pot, scraping the bottom and sides of the pot as you do. Add thyme, marjoram, bay leaves, salt and pepper. Bring to a rapid boil for 10 minutes, then lower heat to medium-low. Simmer for an hour and fifteen minutes to an hour and a half, to reduce it by about one-third.

4 Strain stock through a sieve or china cap to remove bones, etc., then strain again to make smooth. Return sauce to medium heat and stir in currant jelly and sour cream until blended thoroughly. Adjust seasonings.

VENISON MEDALLIONS

4 slices of sirloin of venison 4-6 oz.
Salt and pepper to taste

1 tbs. peanut oil
1 1/2 cups sauce, above

1 Place venison slices, one at a time, between two sheets of thick plastic (a food storage bag is perfect). Pound with the smooth side of a meat mallet until the venison approximately doubles in circumference. Salt and pepper lightly.

2 Heat the oil in a large skillet and saute the venison in hot oil for 45 seconds or so on each side. It cooks very quickly! Drain off excess oil.

3 Serve one slice of venison per person with four ounces of sauce.

Serves four.

Petto Di Tachino Vicenza
Turkey Breast With Olives And Peppers

8 oz. turkey breast, cut in strips
1 tsp. olive oil
1/2 cup dry red wine
1 tsp. chopped onion
1/4 tsp. chopped garlic
1/2 cup chicken stock
8 medium black olives, sliced
1/2 cup mixed red and green bell pepper, chopped
6 whole mushrooms, sliced
1 celery stalk, chopped fine (about 1/4 cup)
1 carrot, chopped fine (about one Tbs.)
1/4 tsp. salt
1/8 tsp. pepper
1 cup angel hair pasta, cooked al dente

1 In a very hot skillet, saute turkey strips in olive oil. Add red wine and reduce for about 10 minutes. Remove the turkey.

2 In the same skillet, saute onion and garlic. Add chicken stock, black olives, bell peppers, mushrooms, celery and carrots. Bring to a boil, then simmer for an additional 10 minutes.

3 Serve over angel hair pasta cooked al dente.
Serves four.

NUTRITION INFORMATION PER SERVING
222 calories
7 gm. fat
2 gm. saturated fat
121 mg. sodium

Petti Di Pollo Parmigiana

Chicken Parmesan

1 tsp. olive oil
2 4-oz. chicken breasts, skinless and boneless
1/4 cup tomato basil sauce (see page 00)
2 oz. part-skim mozzarella
2 slices eggplant (about 1/4 inch thick)
1 cup angel hair pasta, cooked al dente

1 Dust chicken breast with flour and saute in olive oil (saute one side only) for about four minutes—until top part begins to turn white.

2 Rub a little olive oil on each side of the eggplant slices and place on a hot grill for about two minutes each side. (Note: The eggplant should not be breaded.)

3 Layer on a metal dish that can be placed under the broiler the eggplant, the chicken (cooked side down), the tomato sauce, then the mozzarella.

4 Bake at 450 degrees under the broiler for five minutes.

5 Serve either on top of one cup of cooked angel hair pasta or with the pasta on the side.

Serves two.

NUTRITION INFORMATION PER SERVING
475 calories
12 gm. fat
4 gm. saturated fat
261 mg. sodium

Pollo Di Vesuvio

Chicken Steamed With Peppers And Tomatoes

2 4-oz. chicken breasts, skinless, boneless
Flour
1/8 tsp. black pepper
1/2 Tbs. extra virgin olive oil
2 cloves garlic
1/2 tsp. crushed red pepper
1/2 cup red bell pepper, coarsely chopped
1 cup Italian plum tomatoes, chopped
1/2 cup white wine
1 tsp. fresh oregano, chopped
1 tsp. Italian parsley, chopped
1/4 tsp. salt

1 Dust chicken breasts with flour and pepper and bake at 450 degrees for 10 minutes. Remove chicken from oven and keep warm.

2 Saute olive oil, garlic, crushed red pepper and red bell pepper until tender. Add the tomatoes, wine, spices and herbs and cook until well blended.

3 Place chicken breast on serving plate. Top with sauce. Angel hair pasta may be served underneath the chicken breast or on the side.
Serves two.

NUTRITION INFORMATION PER SERVING
285 calories
7 gm. fat
1 gm. saturated fat
450 mg. sodium

Pollo Fiorentino

Chicken Florentine

1 tsp. vegetable oil
4 oz. chicken breast, boneless, skinless
1 tsp. margarine
1 tsp. chopped garlic
1 cup fresh spinach
Pinch of crushed red pepper
1/4 cup skimmed evaporated milk
Pinch salt
1/2 tsp. Parmesan cheese
1/2 oz. part-skim mozzarella cheese

1   Dust skinless, boneless chicken breast with flour. In a skillet under medium heat, saute one side of the chicken breast in oil for 2-3 minutes. Next, turn the chicken breast over to the other side and place in a preheated oven at 450 degrees for five minutes.

2   Wash the spinach well and cook in a little water until it turns tender.

3   In a second pan, saute the margarine, garlic, spinach and crushed red pepper for approximately two minutes.

4   In a third pan, a saucepan, bring the skimmed evaporated milk to a boil. Reduce heat. Add the salt, Parmesan cheese and mozzarella cheese.

5   Assemble serving plate with the chicken breast resting on the bed of spinach topped with the cheese sauce.

6   Serve with your favorite pasta and vegetable.
Serves one.

NUTRITION INFORMATION PER SERVING
351 calories
13 gm. fat
4 gm. saturated fat
330 mg. sodium

Filetto Di Manzo Cacciatore

Filet Of Beef Hunter's Style

1 tsp. canola oil
4 oz. filet mignon
2 whole mushrooms, sliced
1 Italian plum tomato, chopped
1/2 Tbs. onion, chopped
1/2 tsp. garlic, chopped
1/4 cup red wine
2 sprigs parsley
1 sprig rosemary
1/2 tsp. salt

1   In a hot skillet saute the filet mignon in canola oil approximately two minutes on each side. Remove filet mignon from the skillet and place in a preheated 450-degree oven for 10 minutes to cook the meat medium to medium rare.

2   In the same skillet you used to saute the meat, add the mushrooms, tomatoes, onion and garlic and saute for 2-3 minutes.

3   Add the wine, parsley, rosemary and salt and bring to a boil. Reduce the liquid by about two-thirds.

4   Remove the filet from the oven onto a serving dish and top with this sauce.

Serves one.

NUTRITION INFORMATION PER SERVING
300 calories
13 gm. fat
3 gm. saturated fat
512 mg. sodium

Filetto Di Manzo Campagnola

Filet Of Beef With Red Wine

2 4-oz. filet mignons, well trimmed
1 tsp. canola oil
2 tsp. chopped garlic
1 Tbs. chopped onion
2 anchovies, chopped
1/2 cup red and green bell peppers, chopped
1/2 cup red wine
2 fresh mushrooms, sliced
2 sprigs fresh Italian parsley
4 black olives, lightly crushed
1/4 tsp. black pepper

1 In a skillet, heat canola oil and saute steaks until cooked to the desired degree of doneness. Remove filets from pan and keep warm.

2 In the same skillet, cook garlic, onion, anchovy, and peppers until the onions and garlic turn light brown. Add wine, mushroom, parsley, olives and pepper. Cook until two-thirds of the liquid has evaporated.

3 Remove from heat and serve over filet mignon.
Serves two.

NUTRITION INFORMATION PER SERVING
276 calories
11 gm. fat
3 gm. saturated fat
196 mg. sodium

Costoletto Di Maiale Agrodolce
Sweet And Sour Pork Chops

1 Tbs. canola oil
4 pork chops, about 4 oz. each, trimmed of excess fat
2 garlic cloves
1/4 large onion, cubed
1/2 large carrot, sliced in rounds
1 celery stalk chopped with leaves on
1 1/2 cup white wine
1 tomato, diced
1/4 cup balsamic vinegar

Sauce:
1/2 cup pineapple juice
1/4 cup apple juice
1 tsp. salt and pepper
2 Tbs. plain low-fat yogurt
2 Tbs. brown sugar

1   Heat oil in a skillet over medium high heat. When hot, saute the pork chops until browned on one side—approximately eight to ten minutes. Turn the pork chops over and cook for another five or six minutes. Remove and keep warm.

2   Drain excess fat from the pan. Add garlic, onion, carrot, and celery. Saute over medium high heat until brown. Add white wine and bring to a boil. Reduce the wine by two-thirds.

3   Add tomato, vinegar and 1/4 cup water, and return to a boil. Reduce heat to medium and simmer for five minutes.

4   In a second skillet, heat brown sugar, stirring constantly, until it becomes a thick paste. Add juices and yogurt. Blend well and heat through.

5   Strain the sauce from the first pan into the second pan and whisk together. Spoon the sauce over each pork chop. Garnish with pineapple chunks, apple slices, celery leaves, or a dill pickle.
   Serves four.

NUTRITION INFORMATION PER SERVING
401 calories
14 gm. fat
5 gm. saturated fat
153 mg. sodium

Vitello Al Marsala

Veal Marsala

The best veal is white. It comes from calves which are still consuming only their mother's milk. As soon as the animal starts eating grass, the meat gets darker and changes drastically in character. It's still good, but it doesn't have the delicate flavor or tenderness of white veal. The highly distinctive ruddy-brown Marsala wine sauce is the perfect partner for veal.

1 tsp. margarine
Sprinkles of salt, pepper and flour
2 slices white veal scallops

Sauce:
1 1/2 tsp. margarine
1 1/2 tsp. chopped onions
1/8 tsp. chopped garlic
2 large mushrooms, sliced
1/8 cup dry Marsala
1/8 cup dry white wine
1/4 cup demi-glace (see recipe on page 00)
1/8 tsp. salt
Pinch black pepper

1 Dust veal scallops very lightly with salt, pepper and flour.

2 Heat skillet very hot. Put half of the margarine into the skillet and swirl it around. Saute veal for 45 seconds on each side. Remove from skillet and keep warm. Add the rest of the margarine if necessary to finish sauteing all the veal.

3 Make the sauce in the same skillet to get the veal juices. Heat the margarine in the skillet until it bubbles. Add onions and garlic and saute until translucent.

4 Add mushrooms and saute until tender. Add Marsala and white wine and bring to a boil. Reduce for two minutes, stirring occasionally. Add demi-glace, return to a boil and add salt and pepper to taste. Sauce will be rather light in consistency.

Serves two.

NUTRITION INFORMATION PER SERVING
186 calories
10 gm. fat
3 gm. saturated fat
150 mg. sodium

Sides

Asparagi Piccata

Asparagus With Lemon-Mustard Sauce

24 asparagus stalks

Sauce:
1/2 cup low-fat yogurt
1/2 Tbs. Dijon mustard
1/2 tsp. lemon juice
1/2 tsp honey
1/2 tsp. onion juice
Pinch salt
4 drops Tabasco

1   Bring a large saucepan of water to a boil. Wrap asparagus stalks with string and place in boiling water, uncovered, cut end down. Steam for five minutes.

2   While the asparagus is steaming, prepare the sauce. In a saucepan over medium heat, heat yogurt until smooth. Remove from heat and add all the other ingredients. Mix well.

3   Arrange six stalks of asparagus on each plate. Spoon two Tbs. yogurt sauce across the middle of the stalks. Garnish with fresh oregano and tomato slice if desired. This dish may be served hot or cold.
Serves four.

NUTRITION INFORMATION PER SERVING
36 calories
Less than 1 gm. fat
0 gm. saturated fat
97 mg. sodium

Asparagi Milanese

Broiled Asparagus

24 medium asparagus stalks
1 tsp. margarine
1 Tbs. grated Parmesan cheese

Preheat oven to 450 degrees.
1   Bring a large pot of water to a boil. While waiting, cut off the woody ends of the asparagus, and peel the lower portion if necessary with a vegetable peeler. Wrap the asparagus in string and stand up (or lean) the asparagus, tips up, in the boiling water. Steam for 10 minutes.

2   Remove string and spread asparagus out on a baking pan.

3   Melt the margarine and spoon it over the asparagus. Sprinkle the Parmesan cheese over the asparagus. (For best effect, leave the tips bare.)

4   Bake the asparagus in a 450-degree preheated oven until the cheese begins to brown slightly.

Serves four.

NUTRITION INFORMATION PER SERVING
39 calories
1 gm. fat
0 gm. saturated fat
45 mg. sodium

Spinaci Regina

Sauteed Spinach

10 oz. fresh spinach
1 tsp. extra-virgin olive oil
1/4 cup chopped onion
1 Tbs. chopped garlic
1 tsp. crushed red pepper
1/8 tsp. salt

1   Pick the stems from the spinach, then wash the spinach leaves very well in several changes of cold water. Drain.

2   Heat the olive oil in a skillet. When hot, saute the onions, garlic, and crushed red pepper until the onions turn a light blond.

3   Add the spinach, along with 1/4 cup water and the salt. Cook until the spinach wilts—about 15 minutes.

Serves four 1/2-cup servings.

NUTRITION INFORMATION PER SERVING
31 calories
1 gm. fat
0 gm. saturated fat
111 mg. sodium

Verdure Misto

Autumn Vegetable Medley

1/2 eggplant, cut into cubes
1 tsp. salt
1 tsp. canola oil
4 large mushrooms
1/2 red bell pepper, coarsely chopped
1/2 green bell pepper, coarsely chopped
1 yellow squashes, cubed
1 zucchini, cubed
1 tsp. extra-virgin olive oil
1 Tbs. chopped garlic
1/4 cup chopped onion
1 cup dry red wine
2 bay leaves
4 fresh Italian plum tomatoes, cut into cubes
1 tsp. fresh oregano, chopped
1/4 tsp. salt
1/8 tsp. white pepper

1 Sprinkle salt over the eggplant. Place eggplant in a colander, and fit a bowl slightly smaller than the colander into it. Weigh the bowl down with a can from your pantry, and place this whole apparatus into your sink. After about 30 minutes, rinse all the salt off the eggplant and drain well. (This procedure removes the bitterness from eggplants.)

2 Heat the canola oil in a skillet until it begins to ripple. Saute all the vegetables, adding them to the pan in the order listed.

3 In a second skillet, heat extra virgin olive oil until it ripples. Saute the garlic and onion until the onions turn clear. Add the red wine and bay leaves, and bring to a boil. Reduce the red wine for about five minutes, then add the tomatoes. Remove the pan from the heat.

4 Add all the vegetables from the other skillet. Add the oregano, salt and pepper. Toss gently to combine everything, and serve.

Serves eight to ten.

NUTRITION INFORMATION PER SERVING
54 calories
1 gm. fat
0 gm. saturated fat
42 mg. sodium

Broccoli Primavera

Broccoli With Spring Vegetables

1 bunch broccoli
1 lb. fresh asparagus spears, medium
4 large, firm tomatoes
Salt
2 Tbs. fresh chopped oregano
3 Tbs. margarine
1 clove garlic, pressed or pureed
1/4 cup grated Parmesan cheese

Preheat oven to 450 degrees.

1 Heat a large saucepan of water to a boil. While waiting, cut the stems off broccoli at the points where the florets branch off. Cut asparagus spears two inches from the tips. Save the large stems of both vegetables to make soup.

2 Boil asparagus and broccoli together for 20 minutes. Remove and plunge into ice water to arrest cooking and retain the green color.

3 Cut the tomatoes in half. Remove the inside part including all the seeds, but leave the "meat" of the tomato next to the skin. Sprinkle a pinch of salt and some fresh chopped oregano inside each tomato.

4 Arrange four asparagus spears inside the tomato, pointing up at an angle. Fill the center with broccoli florets.

5 In a small saucepan, melt 2 Tbs. margarine until it bubbles. Add the garlic and cook for about two minutes, then remove from the heat.

6 Brush the tops of the broccoli and asparagus with some of the garlic margarine. Sprinkle Parmesan cheese over each.

7 Melt 1 Tbs. margarine in a skillet and place the stuffed tomatoes in it. Put the skillet in the preheated 450-degree oven and bake for 15-20 minutes, until the cheese forms a crust.

Serves four.

NUTRITION INFORMATION PER SERVING
17 calories
0 gm. fat
0 gm. saturated fat
23 mg. sodium

Patate
Parsleyed Potatoes

2 large potatoes, peeled, each cut into eight pieces
1 tsp. margarine
1 Tbs. chopped onion
1 tsp. chopped garlic
2 Tbs. chopped Italian parsley

1   Bring a saucepan of water to a boil and boil the potatoes for about 20 minutes. Drain.
2   In a skillet, heat the margarine until it sizzles. Saute the onions and garlic until they become soft, then add the parsley. Cook for a minute more, than toss the potatoes with the pan contents. Do not brown.
Serves eight.

NUTRITION INFORMATION PER SERVING
64 calories
Less than 1 gm. fat
0 gm. saturated fat
15 mg. sodium

Patate Cabernet
Potatoes Cabernet

1 cup dry red wine
2 medium-large potatoes, peeled and cut in half
1 bay leaf
4 leaves fresh basil, chopped

Preheat oven to 450 degrees.
1   In a saucepan, bring the red wine to a boil. Add the potatoes and the bay leaf.
2   Move the saucepan to the 450 degree oven and bake for one hour. Turn the potatoes every 20 minutes, and add a little water if the pot starts to dry out.
3   Sprinkle with chopped basil and serve.
Serves four.

NUTRITION INFORMATION PER SERVING
71 calories
0 gm. fat
0 gm. saturated fat
40 mg. sodium

Cavolofiore Vesuvia
Steamed Cauliflower

1 head cauliflower
1 tsp. extra-virgin olive oil
1 Tbs. chopped onion
1 tsp. chopped garlic
1/2 chopped red bell pepper
1/2 tsp. dried oregano
1 Tbs. grated Parmesan cheese

1   Bring a large saucepan of water to a boil. While waiting for the bubbles, wash the cauliflower and remove the stem core. Boil the cauliflower for 20 minutes. Remove and drain.

2   In a skillet, heat the olive oil and saute the onion, garlic, red bell pepper, and oregano for just two minutes, then remove from the heat.

3   Sprinkle Parmesan cheese over the top of the cauliflower, and then spread the pan contents over the cauliflower.
Serves four to six.

NUTRITION INFORMATION PER SERVING
50 calories
2 gm. fat
0 gm. saturated fat
47 mg. sodium

Funghi Saltati
Sauteed Mushrooms

1 tsp. margarine
1 Tbs. chopped onion
1/2 tsp. chopped garlic
10 large mushrooms, cut in quarters
1/3 cup white wine
Juice of one lemon
1/8 tsp. dried oregano

1   Heat the margarine in a skillet until it bubbles. Add the onion, garlic, and mushrooms, and cook until the onions turn soft.

2   Add the white wine, lemon juice and oregano. Simmer over medium heat until mushrooms have softened and most of the liquid is absorbed.
Serves four.

NUTRITION INFORMATION PER SERVING
30 calories
Less than 1 gm. fat
0 gm. saturated fat
24 mg. sodium

Fagiolini Anacapri
Green Beans With Garlic

1/2 lb. fresh green beans
Pinch baking soda
1 tsp. extra virgin olive oil
1/2 Tbs. chopped onion
1/2 tsp. chopped garlic
1/8 tsp. crushed red pepper
2 ripe Italian plum tomatoes, chopped
Salt and pepper

1   Bring a large saucepan of water to a boil. While waiting, remove stems and strings, if any, from sides of green beans. Boil green beans, uncovered, with baking soda added to the water (this helps retain the green color). Cook for six to eight minutes, then remove beans and plunge them into ice water.

2   Heat the olive oil in a skillet. Add the onion, garlic, and crushed red pepper. Saute until the onions turn clear.

3   Add the tomatoes and the green beans. Cook until warmed through. Add salt and pepper to taste.

Serves four.

NUTRITION INFORMATION PER SERVING
40 calories
1 gm. fat
0 gm. saturated fat
15 mg. sodium

Zucchini Ripieni

Stuffed Zucchini

1 tsp. margarine
1 Tbs. onion, chopped
1 tsp. chopped garlic
1 large zucchini
2 large mushrooms, chopped
2 Italian plum tomato, chopped
1 tsp. oregano (dried)
1/4 tsp. salt
1/8 tsp. pepper
3 Tbs. red wine
1 Tbs. Parmesan cheese

Preheat oven to 450 degrees.

1   Heat the margarine in a skillet until it bubbles. Saute the onions and garlic for about a minute.

2   Add the mushrooms and saute for about two minutes. Add the tomatoes, oregano, salt and pepper. Cook until the tomatoes are soft.

3   Add the red wine. Cook until most of it has been absorbed, then add the Parmesan cheese. Remove from the heat.

4   Cut zucchini in quarters. With a spoon, dig a hollow in the center of each to make four "boats"

5   Stuff the hollow of each boat with the skillet mixture.

6   Place the stuffed zucchini halves in a baking pan with 1/2 cup of water. Bake the zucchini for 10-12 minutes in the preheated 450-degree oven.

Serves four.

NOTE. The stuffing used above can also be used to stuff tomatoes, large mushrooms, small eggplants, or small squash.

NUTRITION INFORMATION PER SERVING
33 calories
1 gm. fat
0 gm. saturated fat
172 mg. sodium

Zucca Al Spaghetti

Spaghetti Squash

1 spaghetti squash
Vegetable oil spray (i.e., Pam)
1 tsp. extra-virgin olive oil
1 Tbs. chopped onion
1 tsp. chopped garlic
Salt and pepper
1 tsp. thyme

Preheat oven to 450 degrees.

1 Cut the spaghetti squash in half from end to end. Scrape out the seeds in the center.

2 Spray the vegetable oil in a large skillet. Place the spaghetti squash cut side down in the skillet. Move the skillet into the preheated 450-degree oven. Bake for 45 minutes. Remove the squash from the skillet and allow to cool.

3 Using a fork, scrape the squash out of the skin. (You will now discover why it's called "spaghetti squash.")

4 Wipe out the skillet and in it heat the extra-virgin olive oil until it ripples. Saute the onion and garlic for about a minute, then add the squash, salt and pepper to taste, and thyme. Stir the squash around in the skillet to blend all the ingredients.

Serves four to six.

NUTRITION INFORMATION PER SERVING
70 calories
1 gm. fat
0 gm. saturated fat
59 mg. sodium

Zucche Tricolori Saltati

Sauteed Three-Color Squash

1 tsp. extra virgin olive oil
1 Tbs. chopped onion
1 tsp. chopped garlic
3 medium yellow squash, chopped
1/2 red bell pepper, chopped
1/2 green bell pepper, chopped
1 Tbs. fresh basil or 1 tsp. dry basil
1/4 tsp. salt
1/8 tsp. pepper

1   Heat the olive oil in a skillet until it shimmers. Saute the onions and garlic for about a minute.

2   Add the squash and bell peppers. (And basil, if using dried.) Saute for 6-8 minutes, until everything has softened but not until it starts to fall apart.

3   Add salt and pepper to taste, along with fresh basil.
Serves four.

NUTRITION INFORMATION PER SERVING
34 calories
1 gm. fat
0 gm. saturated fat
109 mg. sodium

Crema Di Patate Dolce

Sweet Potato Custard

2 medium sweet potatoes, peeled and diced
2 eggs
2 egg whites
1 cup low-fat milk
1/4 tsp. nutmeg
1/4 tsp. cinnamon
3 Tbs. brown sugar
1 Tbs. white granulated sugar
4 tsp. molasses
8 strawberries

Preheat oven to 350 degreees.

1 Boil the sweet potatoes until tender—about 30 minutes. Scrape them out of their skins and mash them in a bowl.

2 Add all the remaining ingredients except molasses and strawberries. Blend well.

3 Spray four six-ounce custard cups with vegetable oil spray (i.e., Pam). Fill the custard cups with the mixture. Place the cups in a pan of warm water, about 1/2 up the sides of the cups.

4 Bake the custard, in their water bath, in the preheated 350-degree oven for 50 minutes. When finished baking, cool for 10-15 minutes.

5 Invert custard cups onto individual dessert plates. Drizzle 1 tsp. molasses over each custard. Garnish with sliced strawberries.

Serves four.

NUTRITION INFORMATION PER SERVING
210 calories
4 gm. fat
3 gm. saturated fat
101 mg. sodium

Bread Rolls

2 Lbs. whole wheat flour
1 Lb. 00 soft wheat flour
1 oz. instant Yeast
1 oz. salt
Pinch Sugar
2 oz. shortening or olive oil
4 cups of water

1   Add all dry ingredients together in food processor. Mix well using dough blade.

2   Add water 1/2 cup at a time stirring after each addition until all water has been incorporated. Knead for ten minutes.

3   Add shortening or oil, mix well.

4   Remove from mixing bowl. Place on board or table. Let rest for 20 minutes.

5   Form shape of your preference. Let rise for 30 minutes in warm spot.

6   Bake in preheated oven at 425 degrees for 20 minutes or until golden brown.

Makes 48 small 1 oz. rolls or 4 large loaves

Salad

Insalata De Pasta Quattro Stagione
Pasta Salad "Four Seasons"

3 cups (uncooked) corkscrew pasta – preferably three or more colors
1/3 head cauliflower florets
1/3 red bell pepper, seeded and cut into strips
1/3 green bell pepper, seeded and cut into strips
4 mushrooms, sliced
3 cloves garlic
1 tbs. capers, crushed
1/4 small onion, sliced
2 sprigs fresh oregano
6 leaves chopped fresh basil
4 cherry tomatoes, quartered
8 pitted black olives, sliced
1 tsp. salt
1/4 tsp. white pepper
1 green onion, chopped
3 sprigs italian parsley, chopped
1 oz. part-skim mozzarella, shredded
1 tbs. grated Parmesan cheese
1 tbs. extra virgin olive oil
1 tbs. balsamic vinegar
1 steamed baby artichoke heart (canned is okay), cut into quarters
2 radishes, sliced
1/4 cucumber, sliced
1/2 fennel bulb, coarsely chopped
6 lettuce leaves

1   Cook the pasta al dente, then plunge it into ice water. Drain very well and put into a large bowl.
2   Using the same water you cooked the pasta in, boil the cauliflower for eight minutes. Remove, rinse with cold water, and add to the bowl with the pasta. Add peppers and mushrooms.
3   Crush the garlic in a garlic press. Add garlic and capers to bowl.
4   Add all the other ingredients except the lettuce leaves and toss well. There should be no runoff of liquid at the bottom of the bowl, but all parts of the salad should be well-coated with the oil and vinegar.
5   Place six lettuce leaves in the bottom of six glass bowls. Serve two cups of pasta salad per person as a luncheon entree. Garnish with fresh basil.

Serves six.

NUTRITIONAL INFORMATION PER SERVING
210 Calories
9 gm. fat
2 gm. of saturated fat
400 mg. sodium

Insalata Di Spinaci Agrodolce

Sweet and Sour Spinach Salad

1 Tbs. extra virgin olive oil
4 slices turkey bacon, chopped
1/2 small onion, sliced julienne
1/2 Tbs. chopped garlic
1 1/2 Tbs. brown sugar
2 Tbs. balsamic vinegar
1 Tbs. white vinegar
1 tsp. honey
1 tsp. Dijon mustard
1 lb. fresh spinach, washed and trimmed
Salt and pepper to taste

1 Heat olive oil in a skillet. Saute the turkey bacon until translucent.

2 Add the onions, and garlic and saute until light brown at the edges.

3 Add the brown sugar, vinegars, 1 Tbs. cold water, honey, and Dijon mustard. Cook until everything in the pan is about the color of coffee.

4 Remove the skillet from the heat and add the spinach. With a fork, toss the spinach with the sauce until all the leaves are coated. Be careful not to get the spinach too hot. You want it slightly warm, but still firm. Season with salt and pepper and serve warm.

5 If by mistake you overcook this until the leaves are limp, just call it a side vegetable. It may not qualify as a salad, but it still tastes great.

Serves four.

NUTRITION INFORMATION PER SERVING
137 calories
6 gm. fat
1 gm. saturated fat
130 mg. sodium

Insalata D'Anatra

Duck Salad

1/2 roasted duckling
1 Tbs. balsamic vinegar
1 Tbs. extra virgin olive oil
1/2 Tbs. Dijon mustard
1/2 cup chopped apples
1/2 Tbs. honey
1/4 cup sun-dried tomato, cut into strips
1 Tbs. roasted pine nuts
1 Tbs. chopped onion
1 Tbs. chopped garlic
2 sprigs celery leaves, chopped
1/4 cup Major Grey's chutney
1/2 tsp. salt
1/4 tsp. white pepper
1/4 tsp. soy sauce
Juice of 1/2 lemon
1 head Boston lettuce

1 Remove bones and skin from duck. With the smooth side of a meat mallet, smack the pieces of duck meat to flatten them somewhat. This will make it easy to slice thinly.

2 Mix the vinegar, mustard and oil in a large bowl. Stir in the duck strips and all the other ingredients, one at a time in order.

3 Serve the duck mixture atop crisp, cold leaves of romaine and Boston lettuce or chop lettuce coarsely and toss with duck.

Serves two entrees or four appetizers.

NUTRITION INFORMATION PER SERVING
205 calories
11 gm. fat
3 gm. saturated fat
342 mg. sodium

Insalata Luigi Veronelli

Arugula, Endive and Radicchio Salad

1 head Belgian endive
1 head radicchio
2 cups arugula leaves, large stems removed
1 Tbs. cup toasted pine nuts
1 Tbs. Dijon mustard
1 Tbs. balsamic vinegar
1 Tbs. extra virgin olive oil
1/2 tsp. salt
Pinch white pepper

1   Arrange four endive leaves into an X on a large plate. Place three leaves of radicchio on top in the center. Place arugula leaves in between the endive leaves. Top each salad with toasted pine nuts.

2   Combine mustard and vinegar. Add olive oil in a small stream while stirring briskly in one circular direction only. (It helps greatly to have one person pour while the other person stirs.) Stir in 2 Tbs. cold water, salt and pepper.

3   Sauce each salad with two ounces of the dressing and serve.
Serves four.

NUTRITION INFORMATION PER SERVING
73 calories
5 gm. fat
Less than 1 gm. saturated fat
311 mg. sodium

Insalata De Frutti De Mare

Seafood Salad Portofino

1/2 lb. scallops
1 lb. squid, cleaned
1 lb. shrimp, peeled and deveined
1 lb. red snapper fillets
1 1/2 lbs. mussels, in shell
1 1/2 lbs. clams, in shell
1/2 lb. lump crabmeat
1 Tbs. vinegar
2 bay leaves
1 cup water
2 tsp. chopped onion
1 tsp. chopped garlic
1/4 tsp. crushed red pepper
1/4 tsp. salt
1/4 tsp. white pepper
1/2 cup dry white wine
1 head romaine or Bibb lettuce

Sauce:

1 Tbs. extra virgin olive oil
1/4 cup lemon juice
1/2 cup dry white wine
1/2 Tbs. Worcestershire
1/4 cup chopped Italian parsley
1 1/2 tsp. chopped garlic
2 tsp. chopped onion

1   Wash all the seafoods separately.

2   Bring a gallon of water to a boil with the vinegar and the bay leaves. Poach the scallops, squid, shrimp, and snapper, one seafood at a time, for five minutes each, or until the water returns to a boil after the seafood is added. Remove the seafood, drain, and refrigerate.

3   To cook the mussels and clams, heat the water in a large skillet until very hot. Saute the onions and garlic until lightly browned. Add crushed red pepper, salt and pepper. Put the mussels into the pan and pour the wine over them. Bring the wine to a boil and cover the pan. Cook the mussels until they gape open—about five minutes.

4   Remove the mussels from the pan and repeat the same procedure with the clams. Refrigerate the mussels and clams. When cold, remove about half of the mussels and clams from their shells, and chop them coarsely.

5   Whisk together all the sauce ingredients in a large bowl. Add all the seafoods (including the crabmeat, which needs no advance preparation). Toss lightly with the sauce until well coated. Serve the seafood atop the lettuce, surrounded by mussels and clams in the shells.

Serves 12.

NUTRITION INFORMATION PER SERVING
270 calories
8 gm. fat
1 gm. saturated fat
300 mg. sodium

Insalata De Pollo Livornese

Chicken Breast Salad Livornese

2 chicken breasts, cut into medium dice
1 Tbs. chopped onion
1/2 Tbs. chopped garlic
6 pitted black olives, broken
1 medium tomato, cut up
1 Tbs. sun-dried tomatoes, sliced julienne
6 medium mushrooms, sliced
1/2 Tbs. capers
3 anchovies
1 Tbs. extra virgin olive oil
1/2 tsp. salt
1/8 tsp. Tabasco
4 chopped fresh basil leaves
1 sprig fresh oregano leaves, chopped
1 head romaine lettuce, washed, outer leaves removed
2 Tbs. balsamic vinegar
1/4 cup extra virgin olive oil

1   The chicken breasts can be cooked almost any way you like: boiled, broiled, or grilled. To keep the fat low, remove the skin before cooking. After cooking, remove the bones and chop the meat into quarter-inch dice.

2   With a garlic press, puree the onion, garlic, and anchovies.

3   Combine the puree with all other ingredients above through the oregano. Blend well. Divide into four portions.

4   Slice the romaine crosswise about an inch wide. Toss it with the balsamic vinegar and 1/4 cup extra virgin olive oil. Divide it on plates and top each plate with a portion of the chicken mixture.

Serves four.

NUTRITION INFORMATION PER SERVING
150 calories
6 gm. fat
1 gm. saturated fat
70 mg. sodium

Insalata d'Indivia Belga "Aurora"

Belgian Endive Salad Aurora

3 heads Belgian endive
1/2 cup light mayonnaise
1/2 tsp. Worcestershire sauce
1/4 tsp. Tabasco
1/2 tsp. brandy
1/4 tsp. salt
1 Tbs. catsup
Lettuce leaves and red bell pepper for garnish

1   Pull off the discolored or damaged outer leaves of the endives. Slice the heads of endive from top to bottom. With a sharp tapered knife, cut out the stem core. Pull the endive halves apart and wash well. Dry the leaves inside a towel or with a salad spinner. Reserve 16 of the best-looking leaves. Cut the rest of the leaves across into five or so pieces.

2   Arrange four of the nice, whole leaves in an X on the plate.

3   In a large bowl, combine the mayonnaise, Worcestershire, Tabasco, brandy, salt and catsup and mix well. Put the cut-up endives into the sauce and toss. It will seem like there is way too much dressing, but the residue will drip down onto the whole endive leaves on the plate. Spoon the sauce-coated endives onto the center.

4   Garnish with small leaves of green lettuce and strips of red bell pepper.

Serves four.

NUTRITION INFORMATION PER SERVING
100 calories
8 gm. fat
0 gm. saturated fat
217 mg. sodium

Mozzarella Caprese
Mozzarella Salad

1 extra-large ripe tomato
5 oz. part-skim mozzarella cheese
1/2 Tbs. extra virgin olive oil
8 leaves fresh basil, cut in strips
1 Tbs. fresh oregano, chopped
1 Tbs. chopped onion
1 Tbs. chopped garlic
1/4 tsp. salt
1 Tbs. chopped Italian parsley
1 head Boston or Bibb lettuce

1   Clean and cut one large tomato into cubes.
2   Cut part-skim mozzarella into small cubes.
3   Combine the olive oil, 2 Tbs. cold water, fresh herbs and spices together. Add tomatoes and cheese.
4   Serve on bed of crisp Boston lettuce.
Serves five.

NUTRITION INFORMATION PER SERVING
93 calories
6 gm. fat
3 gm. saturated fat
240 mg. sodium

Insalata Di Fagiolini Verdi

Green Bean Salad

1 lb. fresh green beans
1 Tbs. extra virgin olive oil
1 Tbs. chopped garlic
1 1/2 Tbs. chopped onion
6 sprigs Italian parsley, chopped
1/4 tsp. crushed red pepper
1 tsp. balsamic vinegar
Pinch white pepper and salt
1 Tbs. dry white wine

1   Boil one gallon of water with about one tsp. salt in a large saucepan. Drop in the beans. When the water returns to a boil, boil the beans for 15 minutes. Remove and plunge the beans immediately into ice water to cool. Drain well.

2   In a bowl, combine all other ingredients. Add the beans and marinate overnight.

3   Serve as antipasto or as a salad. Garnish with leaves of red lettuce. *Serves four.*

NUTRITION INFORMATION PER SERVING
38 calories
2 gm. fat
0 gm. saturated fat
3 mg. sodium

Insalata Di Finocchi

Fennel Salad

2 bunches fresh fennel
1/4 onion, sliced
1 tsp. extra virgin olive oil
Juice of one lemon
3 cloves garlic, crushed or pressed
2 sprigs Italian parsley
1/4 tsp. salt
Pinch white pepper
2 tsp. white vinegar

1   Cut out the root core of the fennel and cut off most of the length of the stems. (Reserve some of the leaves for garnish.). Pull the bulbs apart and wash very well. Chop into strips.

2   Add all other ingredients and mix well.

3   Cut, wash, and dry small sprigs of the feathery fennel leaves to garnish the salad.

Serves eight.

NUTRITION INFORMATION PER SERVING

15 calories
Less than 1 gm. fat
0 gm. saturated fat
33 mg. sodium

Insalata Di Fave

Fava Bean Salad

1 lb. fava beans
1/2 cup dry white wine
1 Tbs. extra virgin olive oil
1 Tbs. balsamic vinegar
4 bay leaves
1 1/2 tsp. garlic
1/2 small red onion, slivered
6 sprigs Italian parsley, stems removed, chopped
Pinch white pepper and salt

1   Soak fava beans in cool water overnight.
2   Drain and put into a saucepot with one gallon of cold water. Simmer for two hours or until beans are tender but not breaking apart.
3   Drain and allow to cool. Remove skins from beans.
4   In a bowl blend wine, olive oil, and vinegar with a wire whisk. Add bay leaves, garlic, onion, parsley, salt, pepper, and fava beans. Toss ingredients well. Give the beans an hour or two to absorb the sauce, then serve as as antipasto at room temperature.

Serves eight.

NUTRITION INFORMATION PER SERVING
82 calories
3 gm. fat
0 gm. saturated fat
296 mg. sodium

Dessert

Strawberry Yogurt Cake

Sponge Cake:

4 eggs, separated
1/2 cup sugar
1/2 cup hot water
1 1/2 tsp. vanilla extract
1 1/2 tsp. cake flour (sifted)
1/4 tsp. salt
1/4 tsp. baking powder

1   With an electric beater, beat egg yolks and sugar until thick and pale yellow. Slowly beat in hot water and vanilla.
2   Combine cake flour, salt and baking powder in sifter. Sift and stir into egg yolk mixture. Beat egg whites until stiff and fold into egg yolk mixture.
3   Spoon batter into ungreased 9 in. cake pan.
4   Bake at 325 degrees for 30-35 minutes.
5   Invert pan and allow to cool for at least one hour. Using a long, serrated cake knife, cut off the rounded top. Then cut the cake into three layers of equal thickness.

Filling and Icing:

1 cup water
2 cups sugar
2 Tbs. Triple Sec
10 strawberries, sliced
1 cup nonfat vanilla yogurt
1 cup low-fat whipped topping

1   Dissolve the sugar in 1 cup of water in a small saucepan. Heat until lightly boiling, and cook until reduced to 1/2 cup of simple syrup.
2   Combine the syrup and Triple Sec in a bowl and brush it on the top of the bottom layer of sponge cake.
3   Mix the yogurt and low-fat whipped topping together. Spread this mixture onto the sponge cake. Top with sliced strawberries.
4   Place another layer of sponge cake on top of the first. Brush with syrup, spread the filling, and top with strawberries. Complete with the final layer of cake. Brush with syrup and use the remaining filling to cover the top and sides of the cake. Decorate the top with strawberries. Garnish with graham-cracker crumbs on the side.
Serves 16.

NUTRITION INFORMATION PER SERVING
95 calories
1 gm. fat
1 gm. saturated fat
61 mg. sodium

Budino Di Pane

Bread Pudding

12 oz. bread (stale bread is preferable)
5 cups skim milk
2 oz. raisins
4 egg whites
3 whole eggs
1 cup skim milk
1 Tbs. vanilla
1/2 cup sugar
1/2 Tbs. cinnamon
1/4 cup sugar, dissolved in 2 Tbs. water

Sauce:
1 cup nonfat yogurt
1 cup low-fat frozen whipped topping (i.e., Cool Whip)
1 Tbs. vanilla

Preheat oven to 350 degrees.

1   In a deep mixing bowl, break bread into one inch cubes (approximately). Add skim milk and raisins. Blend together with your fingers. Let sit for approximately 10 minutes.

2   Place egg whites, whole eggs, milk, and sugar in another mixing bowl and beat at medium-high speed for five minutes. Add vanilla and cinnamon.

3   Blend the egg mixture into the bread mixture gently.

4   Spread the dissolved sugar on the bottom of a baking dish. Heat in a preheated 350 degrees oven until it browns slightly. Remove the dish from the oven and add the bread mixture.

5   Return the dish to the oven for one and one-half hours, or until a cake tester comes out clean. Remove from oven and let cool.

6   While the bread pudding is baking, prepare the sauce. In a saucepan, heat yogurt over medium heat until smooth. Remove from heat and let cool. Stir in whipped topping and vanilla.

7   Cut the bread pudding into 12 equal servings. Serve with the yogurt sauce on top.

Serves 12.

NUTRITION INFORMATION PER SERVING
218 calories
4 gm. fat
2 gm. saturated fat
250 mg. sodium

Tirami Su

Pick-Me-Up Cake

Genoise (Sponge Cake):

4 eggs, separated
1/2 cup sugar
1 1/2 tsp. vanilla extract
1 1/2 cup cake flour
1/4 tsp. salt
1/4 tsp. baking powder

Preheat oven to 325 degrees.

1   With an electric beater, beat egg yolks and sugar until thick and lemon-colored.

2   Beat in 1/2 cup hot water and vanilla.

3   Combine cake flour, salt and baking powder in sifter. Sift and stir into egg yolk mixture.

4   With a clean beater and bowl, beat egg whites until stiff. Fold into batter.

5   Spoon batter into ungreased 9-in. cake pan. Bake at 325 degrees for 30-35 minutes, or until a cake tester comes out clean. Invert pan on top of a rack and allow to cool for at least one hour.

Cake Filling:

1/2 cup sugar
1 tsp. vanilla
1 cup mascarpone cheese
1/4 cup non-fat dry milk powder
1 tbs. lemon juice
3/4 cup espresso or strong coffee
1 oz. rum or rum extract
2 tbs. cocoa powder

1   Blend sugar and vanilla into the mascarpone cheese.

2   In a separate bowl, gradually blend dry milk powder into 1/4 cup very cold water, beating at high speed with an electric mixer until stiff, like whipped cream. Gently fold in lemon juice.

3   Fold the mascarpone cheese mixture into the whipped topping and continue to whip until stiff. Set aside.

4   In a cup, combine espresso and rum.

5   Cut the rounded top off the sponge cake, then cut the remainder of the cake into three layers of equal thickness.

6   Brush each layer of cake with the espresso mixture. Spread about a half-inch-thick layer of the mascarpone cheese mixture on the bottom layer. Top with the second layer, and repeat procedure for all three layers of cake. Cover the top and side of the cake with the mascarpone cheese mixture.

7   Sprinkle the top and sides of the cake with cocoa powder using a sieve. Refrigerate for at least three hours. The cake should remain refrigerated until serving.

Serves 16.

NUTRITION INFORMATION PER SERVING
275 calories
10 gm. fat
5 gm. saturated fat
203 mg. sodium

Bananas Foster

2 bananas
4 Tbs. dark brown sugar
4 oz. dark rum
1/2 tsp. cinnamon
12 oz. frozen low-fat vanilla yogurt

1   Peel the bananas and slice lengthwise, then crosswise.

2   In a skillet, heat the brown sugar over medium-low heat until it begins to melt. Add the rum and the bananas and bring to a boil, gently tilting the skillet back and forth.

3   Carefully touch a flame to the rum. Cook, continuing to tilt the pan back and forth, until the flame dies out. Lower the heat and cook until the bananas have softened all the way through. Sprinkle the cinnamon into the pan.

4   Divide the frozen yogurt among four bowls. Spoon the bananas and the sauce over the yogurt and serve.

Serves four.

NUTRITION INFORMATION PER SERVING
198 calories
1 gm. fat
1 gm. saturated fat
58 mg. sodium

Torta Nunziale

Wedding Cake

Although the idea of a low-calorie wedding cake is absurd (after all, how many of them will you ever have?), the recipe that we use for wedding cakes at Andrea's can be lightened up for more frequent use. This version is glazed with a light, luscious lemon glaze.

2/3 cups vegetable shortening
1 cup sugar
2 1/4 cups all-purpose flour
3 1/2 tsp. baking powder
1 tsp. salt
1 1/4 cups skim milk
1 tsp. vanilla
1/2 tsp. almond extract
5 egg whites

Preheat oven to 350 degrees.

1   Cream the shortening and sugar together in a large bowl.

2   Sift the dry ingredients together and add them to the bowl about one-fourth at a time, alternating with one-fourth of the milk, while continuing to run the mixer on medium speed. Add vanilla and almond extract.

3   Beat egg whites in a separate, grease-free bowl till stiff but not dry. Fold the beaten egg whites into the cake batter with a spatula or (most effective) with your fingers. Do not overmix. Try to retain the fluffiness of the egg whites.

4   Spoon the batter into cake pans of appropriate size to your idea of a wedding cake. Bake in preheated 350 degree oven for 45 minutes until springy, or until a cake tester inserted into the middle comes out clean. Remove and cool cakes on wire racks.

5   Slice off the tops of the cakes, and then slice the cakes into three layers with a long serrated knife. Spread lemon glaze between the layers and over the cake.

Lemon Glaze

4 fresh lemons
1/4 cup sugar
2 tsp. corn starch

1   Scrape the zest from all the lemons and chop fine. Juice the lemons.

2   Bring 2 cups water to a boil in a saucepan. Add lemon zest, juice, and sugar to a boil. Simmer about 10 minutes.

3   In a small cup, mix one oz. water with two tsp. cornstarch. Add this mixture to the pot and simmer for about two more minutes. Remove from heat and refrigerate until cool. Spread between layers of silver cake and then pour over the entire cake to glaze.

Serves about 50 people.

NUTRITION INFORMATION PER SERVING
67 calories
3 gm. fat
Less than 1 gm. saturated fat
77 mgs. sodium

Pera Affogata

Poached Pears

4 ripe pears, peeled and cored
1/3 cup lemon juice
1/3 cup dry white wine
4 oz. semi-sweet chocolate

1   Put the pears in a bowl with cold water and half of the lemon juice. This will keep the pears from browning as you continue.

2   Bring 1/2 gallon cold water to a boil. Put the pears in as soon as the water starts to roll, along with the rest of the lemon juice and the wine. Boil for 20 minutes, then turn off the heat but leave pears in the hot water.

3   Meanwhile, melt the chocolate in a double boiler over medium-low heat. Pour the chocolate into a measuring cup set in a pan of hot water to keep it warm.

4   After the pears have cooled to lukewarm, dry them and dip them, top down, into the hot melted chocolate in the cup. After the chocolate sets, coat the bottom halves of the pears with chocolate. Refrigerate.

NOTE: Make sure the pears are very dry before you dip them. Even a small amount of water will cause melted chocolate to start lumping up.

5   Serve garnished with mint.

Serves four.

NUTRITION INFORMATION PER SERVING
260 calories
10 gm. fat
6 gm. saturated fat
14 mg. sodium

Sorbetto Al Limone

Lemon Sorbet

Juice of 12 medium lemons
1 Tbs. lemon zest
2 cups sugar dissolved in two cups water

1 Load all the ingredients into an ice cream freezer and run it for 20-30 minutes until you have a thick, thoroughly frozen slurry.

2 Scoop the slurry into a plastic container and freeze until hard.

Makes one quart—about eight servings..

Lemon zest is made by running an inexpensive tool called a "zester" across the skin of the lemon. A cheese grater can also be used. Don't go into the bitter white part of the skin when doing this; all the oils are in the colored exterior.

NUTRITION INFORMATION PER SERVING
205 calories
0 gm. fat
0 gm. saturated fat
0 mg. sodium

Sorbetto Al Calvados

Calvados Sorbet

1 sweet, ripe apple, peeled and cored
1/4 cup Calvados
2 cups sugar dissolved into two cups water

Cut up the apple and puree in a food processor. Combine with other ingredients and proceed as for the lemon sorbet, above.

Makes one quart—about eight servings.

NUTRITION INFORMATION PER SERVING
198 calories
0 gm. fat
0 gm. saturated fat
0 mg. sodium

Rice Pudding

1 egg white
1/2 cup skim milk
1/4 tsp. ground cinnamon
1/4 tsp. ground nutmeg
1/4 tsp. ground allspice
1/4 tsp. vanilla extract
2 Tbsp. raisins
2 pkts. sweet-n-low™ or sweet one™
2/3 cup cooked white rice

Preheat oven to 325 degrees.

1 Beat the egg white with the skim milk.
2 Add the spices, raisins and rice. Gently stir until thoroughly mixed.
3 Bake for 20 minutes. May serve hot or cold.
   Serves two.

NUTRITIONAL INFORMATION PER SERVING
145 Calories
0 gm. fat
1 mg. cholesterol
58 mg. sodium

Red Raspberry Cake

2 cups red raspberries
1/2 cup sugar
3/4 cup water
1-1/2 Tbsp. cornstarch
1 commercially baked angel food cake

1 Combine the berries and sugar in a saucepan and simmer over medium-high heat for about 40 minutes.
2 Lower the heat and mix cornstarch and water. Add this to the sauce and stir until thickened.
3 To serve, take 1/16 of an angel food cake and drizzle raspberry sauce over the top.
   Serves sixteen.

NUTRITIONAL INFORMATION PER SERVING
160 Calories
0 gm. fat
0 mg. cholesterol
140 mg. sodium